BY THE SAME AUTHOR

La Liberté de l'Esprit dans l'Expérience mystique (Paris, Nouvelle Équipe, 1933)

La doctrine de l'intelligence chez Aristote, essai d'exégèse (preface by Étienne Gilson. Paris, Vrin, 1934)

Le Commentaire de Jean Philopon sur le Troisième Livre du "Traité de l'Âme" d'Aristote (Paris, Droz, 1934)

Aristote et Plotin. Études d'histoire de la philosophie ancienne (Paris, Desclée De Brouwer, 1935)

La Philosophie de Gabriel Marcel (Paris, Téqui, 1938)

L'Essence de la poésie. Étude philosophique de l'acte poétique (Brussels, Cahier des Poètes Catholiques, 1942)

Incarnation de l'homme. Psychologie des mœurs contemporaines (Paris, Libraire de Médicis, 1942; reprinted: Brussels, Éditions Universitaires, 1944)

Philosophie des mœurs contemporaines (Brussels, Éditions Universitaires, 1944)

Du fond de l'abîme. Essai sur la situation morale de notre pays au lendemain de la Libération (Bruges, Desclée De Brouwer, 1945)

Essai sur la fin d'une civilisation (Brussels, Éditions Universitaires; Paris, Libraire de Médicis, 1949)

Mon pays où vas-tu? Philosophie et histoire de la crise belge de 1950 (Paris-Brussels, Éditions Universitaires 1951)

(Cowritten with Marie De Corte, his wife) *Deviens ce que tu es: Léon, notre fils, 1937-1955.* (Paris, Éditions Universitaires, 1956; reprinted: Paris, Nouvelles Éditions Latines, 1969)

J'aime le Canada français (Québec, Presses Universitaires Laval, 1960)

L'homme contre lui-même (Paris, Nouvelles Éditions Latines, 1962)

L'intelligence en péril de mort (Paris, Club de la Culture française, 1969; new edition: Paris, Éditions de l'Homme Nouveau, 2017); English edition: *Intelligence in Danger of Death*, Waterloo, Arouca Press, 2023)

De la Justice (Dominique Martin Morin, 1973)

De la prudence. La plus humaine des vertus (Dominique Martin Morin, 1974)

De la force (Dominique Martin Morin, 1980)

De la tempérance (Dominique Martin Morin, 1982)

De la dissociété (Paris, Remi Perrin, 2002)

Descartes, philosophe de la modernité (Paris, Éditions de l'Homme Nouveau, 2022)

ON THE DEATH OF A CIVILIZATION

On the Death
of a
Civilization

MARCEL DE CORTE
Translated by Inez Fitzgerald Storck
Historical Introduction by Thomas Storck

AROUCA
PRESS

To Gabriel Marcel
as a testimony of my affection

CONTENTS

HISTORICAL INTRODUCTION
Thomas Storck

T HE PHILOSOPHICAL AND SOCIAL OUT-
look of such a thinker as the Belgian philosopher
and Liège professor, Marcel De Corte (1905-1994),
can only be understood within the context of the Church's
response to the modern world, and the subsequent Catholic
intellectual revival, which in essence was a reassertion of
the Church's spiritual, intellectual, and social heritage as
an alternative to modernity. This revival, which began
haltingly in the first half of the nineteenth century, reached
its apogee in the 1930s, and petered out sometime after 1960,
frames the thought of De Corte as it has of many another
figure. This revival is marked chiefly by two related features. One is the recovery of the philosophical thought of
Thomas Aquinas, while the second is an approach to the
social order that sets it apart from the general tendencies
of modern thought.

De Corte was explicit about both these points: "I have
not philosophized except through my reading of Aristotle
and St. Thomas Aquinas . . . "[1] he wrote, and as to the second point, readers of the volume in hand, as well as of his
other work published by Arouca Press, *Intelligence in Danger
of Death*, will readily perceive the contours of his critique
of the contemporary social order. Thus De Corte did not
philosophize or speak on social questions in a vacuum. As
I said, he shared a basic orientation with a host of other
thinkers, including even non-Catholics who perceived
both the intellectual bankruptcy of modern philosophy
and the sterile socio-political debates that are endemic

---

1 "Autobiographie philosophique," quoted in Miguel Ayuso, "Marcel De
Corte y el Pensamiento Político Antimoderno," *Verbo*, no. 327-328, 1994,
p. 764. My translation from the Spanish.

to our civilization, as well as our alienation from each other, from the natural world, from all that is authentic to human life. These writers created a powerful response to modern life, a response that seemed to be connatural with the Catholic mind and which for nearly a hundred years gave a distinctive tone to Catholic thought. That this response to modernity was largely abandoned in the mid-twentieth century is one of the greatest tragedies in the history of the Church.

In order to understand this twofold stance of De Corte and of the thinkers of the Catholic revival generally, it is necessary to grasp the radical and immense change which modernity introduced, and its corresponding effect upon Catholics. The Catholic Church existed at first within a Jewish milieu, different from and opposed to the paganism which reigned in the rest of the world. Although the Church, in what has been called the "first wholly fundamental turning point in the history of Christianity," broke out of her original mode of thought and life and entered into an engagement with pagan philosophical thought, an action which made it possible for her to "set out on its missionary journey across the Mediterranean world, and across different nations, ethnic groups, cultural and social strata,"[2] we are entitled to see this change as less fundamental than one might think at first. For in different ways both Hebrew and pagan thought conceived of the universe as a cosmos, an order ruled by unseen powers who controlled the destiny of individuals and nations and to whose will and purpose it was our task to conform ourselves.

The Church understood paganism, as St. Paul's discourse in Acts 17 makes clear, for both Hebrew and Greek milieux were sacral cultures, as was obviously the new culture which the Church herself was in process of creating and which took elements from both the Jewish and gentile

---

2   Tomás Petrácek, *Church, Society and Change* (Lublin: El-Press, 2014), p. 13-14.

cultures. Thus the Church rested securely in the civilization which was coming into being, the product of her own
life and activity, which reached such brilliance during the
High Middle Ages. But equally obviously that civilization
declined, slowly and unevenly, to be sure, but it declined
and it eventually disappeared.

What came after that is modernity, an epoch whose
essence so many have struggled to grasp. However we interpret it, the main point to perceive here is that modernity
came into being largely as a rejection of the culture of
Christendom. The Church did not create this new era and
as a result Catholics struggled to understand it and to mark
out its main features. It was foreign territory. For "Christians and pagans had much more in common with each
other than either has with a post-Christian."[3]

The triumph of the bourgeois parliamentary regime in
England in 1688 and the American revolution of 1775 had
little direct effect on the Catholic world. And despite the
incessant activity of Enlightenment thinkers during the
eighteenth century, even within historic Catholic cultures,

> the broad Catholic laity, as well as most of the Catholic
> clergy and religious, for a long time continued to live in
> social enclaves relatively immune from infection by the
> small subculture of the liberal bourgeois intelligentsia.
> This was particularly so in the case of the still vast Catholic
> peasantry. Further, within Catholicism, even when liberal
> infection did threaten, ecclesial censorship and burning
> of printed books, backed up by repressive Catholic state
> power, held the Enlightenment in check for a long time.[4]

But then the French Revolution occurred, in the heart
of Catholic Europe, an event which overturned the
already decaying Catholic social order built up over more
than a thousand years, and for which the demise of the

---

3   C. S. Lewis, "*De Descriptione Temporum*" in *Selected Literary Essays*
(Cambridge: Cambridge University, 1979), p. 5.
4   Joe Holland, *Modern Catholic Social Teaching: The Popes Confront the
Industrial Age, 1740–1958* (New York: Paulist, c. 2003), p. 35.

thousand-year-old Holy Roman Empire in 1806 may be taken as a symbolic end.

It was understandable that many Catholics, after the final defeat of Napoleon in 1815, wanted nothing more than a return to the pre-1789 social order. And at first it seemed as if something akin to that could be achieved, at least in the political arena. But while under Metternich's sway politics may have been relatively calm until 1848, this was hardly the case in the intellectual realm, where a ferment of new and often contradictory ideas flourished. In addition to the continuing influence of the thought of the eighteenth century, other movements arose in opposition to that. The Romantic movement gave rise to diverse, even contradictory, cultural streams, and in an exaggerated rejection of the Enlightenment's conception of reason, thinkers such as Louis Bautain or Louis Bonald abandoned natural theology as a preamble of faith, and looked instead to a primitive revelation, handed down from Adam, as the ultimate foundation for belief.

During the preceding two centuries or so, many Catholic thinkers had adopted views taken from contemporary philosophical currents, especially those of Descartes, and by early in the eighteenth century "the influence of Descartes' philosophy had penetrated ecclesiastical seminaries in spite of official prohibition and discouragement."[5] Indeed, Leo XIII noted that "systems of philosophy multiplied beyond measure" and that they even "caught the souls of certain Catholic philosophers, who, throwing aside the patrimony of ancient wisdom, chose rather to build up a new edifice than to strengthen and complete the old by aid of the new . . ." (Encyclical *Aeterni Patris*, no. 24). But early in the nineteenth century, chiefly in Italy, Catholic thinkers began to turn to St. Thomas and to the task of gaining or regaining a more complete understanding of his thought

---

5 Frederick Copleston, *A History of Philosophy*, vol. 4 (Garden City, N. Y.: Doubleday, 1963), p. 183.

and of its application to the changed world of modernity, an effort crowned by Pope Leo with his vigorous endorsement of the philosophy of St. Thomas in his *Aeterni Patris* of 1878.

Similarly in the social order new and previously unknown ideas were in the ascendant. Medieval Christendom had conceived of society organically, as akin to a family, with varying roles and duties assigned by nature and custom to different persons. This meant among other things that the economy was not seen as a separated sphere of social life ruled by its own inexorable laws, but as part of a larger whole which included all of human activity. Although the mercantilism of the Baroque Catholic monarchies had in many respects hollowed out the medieval economic order, still there was a sense that the economy ought to serve the common good and that the state had a definite role in bringing this about. The craft guilds had been the lynchpin of the medieval economic order and they continued their activity even into the nineteenth century, especially in Germany, although more and more in a decayed state. The role of the guilds in resisting the advent of capitalism was described by Karl Marx himself in these words:

> The rules of the guild . . . by limiting most strictly the number of apprentices and journeymen that a single master could employ, prevented him from becoming a capitalist. Moreover, he could not employ his journeyman in any other handicraft than the one in which he was a master. The guilds zealously repelled every encroachment by the capital of merchants, the only form of free capital with which they came in contact. A merchant could buy every kind of commodity, but labour as a commodity he could not buy. . . . On the whole, the labourer and his means of production remained closely united, like the snail with its shell, and thus there was wanting the principal basis of manufacture, the separation of the labourer from his means of production, and the conversion of these means into capital. [6]

---

6 *Capital*, chap. 14. In the *Encyclopaedia Britannica* Great Books of the Western World edition (Chicago, 1952), this quote is on p. 175. See also p. 149 (chap. 11).

But with the appearance of the theoreticians of the capitalist order an entirely novel approach to the social order had arisen.

> [L]abour itself was coming to be regarded as 'a commodity exchangeable for benefit', ... This brought labour out of the guild system of solidarity and into the system of exchange; it replaced work or calling as a fixed status, inherited or acquired, with its own 'honour', by occupational mobility and a free market in labour. It legitimized the transition from a guild-based and mercantilist economy to a free-market economy in the full sense; and it enabled the future science of political economy to disregard any rights of labour that were not justifiable in terms of exchange value.[7]

It was the Revolution of 1789 in France which gave this new conception of society free rein in Catholic Europe, abolishing the remnants of the medieval Catholic economic order, allowing the "enclosure of common lands for property-seeking rural entrepreneurs, banning of trade unions among the working class, and abolition of the feudal guilds and corporations of artisan monopolies."[8] As De Corte remarks in this volume, "Trades, stricken in their cohesiveness by the Chapelier Law, are swept into the orbit of an unbridled capitalist economy where the mathematical abstract law of profit above all things holds sway. . . ." (See p. 39) None other than Friedrich Engels described the post-1789 situation in these words:

> The antagonism between rich and poor, instead of dissolving into general prosperity, had become intensified by the removal of the guild and other privileges, which had to some extent bridged it, and by the removal of the charitable institutions of the Church. The "freedom of property" from feudal fetters, now veritably accomplished, turned out to be, for the small capitalists and small proprietors, the freedom to sell their small property, crushed under the overmastering competition of the large capitalists and

7   Antony Black, *Guilds and Civil Society in European Political Thought from the Twelfth Century to the Present* (Ithaca: Cornell University, 1984), p. 154-55.
8   Joe Holland, *Modern Catholic Social Teaching*, p. 37.

landlords, to these great lords, and thus, as far as the small capitalists and peasant proprietors were concerned, became "freedom *from* property."[9]

The new economic order was animated by a very different spirit from that which had prevailed in Christendom, a spirit based in the final instance on a new concept of man himself.

Fundamentally modern political thought rests upon two related concepts, that of the natural solitary individual who enters into a social compact, and as a consequence, that of the state as the only significant human collectivity. We may take John Locke as the representative figure here, for his account of the social contract preceded Rousseau's by half a century and had much more influence than Thomas Hobbes' earlier and more dire version. Locke writes,

> To understand political power aright, and derive it from its original, we must consider what estate all men are naturally in, and that is, a state of perfect freedom to order their actions, and dispose of the possessions and persons as they think fit, within the bounds of the law of Nature, without asking leave or depending upon the will of any other man. [10]

According to this account, in its original and native state human nature is autonomous, men are essentially solitary, free from obligations toward others (except those of the natural law), masters of themselves. It follows from this that any bonds between men must be freely chosen. This is to establish for the first time a contractual society, "one of the greatest upheavals in man's view of himself and the world."[11] For previously it had been obvious to social and political thinkers that human beings, far from being by nature solitary and autonomous, were naturally parts of various social nexus. The political community or *polis* was the natural home of mankind, but within that community

9 "Socialism: Utopian and Scientific" in Karl Marx and Friedrich Engels, *Basic Writings on Politics and Philosophy* (Garden City, N. Y.: Doubleday, 1959), p. 72.
10 *Concerning Civil Government, Second Essay*, no. 4.
11 Antony Black, *Guilds and Civil Society in European Political Thought*, p. 157.

various other communities flourished in an organic whole, as part of a complex of smaller communities.

> [W]ithin the city, the autonomous corporate organization of the different economic activities in the economic and social life of the community, by means of the gild system, corresponds perfectly with the doctrine of the organic differentiation and mutual interdependence of the members of the Christian society. Thus the medieval city was a community of communities in which the same principles of corporate rights and chartered liberties applied equally to the whole and to the parts. For the medieval idea of liberty, which finds it highest expression in the life of the free cities, was not the right of the individual to follow his own will, but the privilege of sharing in a highly organized form of corporate life which possessed its own constitution and rights of self-government. In many cases this constitution was hierarchical and authoritarian, but as every corporation had its own rights in the life of the city, so every individual had his place and his rights in the life of the gild. [12]

Since in Locke's view human beings are essentially autonomous individuals who originally enter voluntarily into civil society and as a result establish a state, the state becomes the only significant and effective corporate body and assumes a more important role in society and its regulation than the medieval state had had. Intermediate groups are no longer natural and organic parts of a whole, but merely voluntary associations whose existence depends upon the desires or whims of their members. Thus as Pope Pius XI put it, "the highly developed social life which once flourished in a variety of prosperous and interdependent institutions, has been damaged and all but ruined, leaving virtually only individuals and the State"[13]

This is the background for De Corte's insistent call for what he terms an organic society. "The distinctive characteristic of a true civilization is to bring together, *organically*,

---

12 Christopher Dawson, *Religion and the Rise of Western Culture*, (New York: Sheed & Ward, 1950), p. 206.
13 Encyclical *Quadragesimo Anno* (1931), no. 78.

with unity in diversity, persons who without it would live as isolated individuals" (See p. 12) The absence of these organic bonds colors all of modern life, in which *"man admits he is incapable of participating in the real world and of working with others organically in a specific community."* (See p. 21)

This lack of organic connections between human persons is based, in De Corte's view, on a prior lack of an organic correspondence with the natural.

> In the living, unified expression which is observed in authentic civilizations, different types of persons participate in it. Here again the analogies with nature are striking. The leaves of a tree are not identical; they only resemble each other. No two are identical in the manner of two geometrical shapes of the same dimensions or two manufactured objects cast in the same mold. The differences among leaves, flowers, fruit, branches, trunk, and root are still more obvious. All the parts of a tree, however, form one organic unity. (See p. 11)

In Lockean thought the natural differences between persons become necessarily unimportant, since each of us is seen as theoretically independent and free, master of himself. The state or civil society is not something organic, that is, akin to an organism with differentiated functioning parts, but like a structure formed of interchangeable manufactured objects. This conception of society and of human life has been a disaster for mankind and is largely the immediate reason for the various dilemmas in which we now find ourselves. Is there any way out, any escape from the strictures which modernity has put upon us?

Whether or not we will actually embrace any exit strategy from modernity, the way has been pointed out to us repeatedly. Writers such as Marcel De Corte are part of a long line of Catholic thinkers who have not only diagnosed the ills of our times but prescribed the appropriate remedies. Will we take advantage of their advice? That is up to us. It is our choice.

What is Civilization?

THE PHENOMENON OF CIVILIZATION energetically resists analysis. Its content is so vast that it is difficult to grasp and to enumerate its elements: religion, the arts, literature, science, customs, and an understanding of existence, all blended together, intertwined, organizing themselves and merging into one another in a huge homogeneous stream. A reciprocal solidarity binds them together and to a totality which escapes any attempt to take hold of it in order to look at it. With civilization it is just as with life itself: it constitutes a unified whole incapable of being broken apart, not only on account of its breadth, but also in virtue of its irreducible character, which means that the whole is not equivalent to the sum of its parts. We know for example the principal elements of Greek civilization. A wealth of research has brought them to light: the investigation is practically completed. Yet, however, the controversy is endless when it comes down to fitting them together. Between Winckelmann's[1] interpretation to Nietzsche's[2] there is an abyss. It is the same with primitive civilizations, which sociologists in their offices specialize in. Everywhere the path stops at the threshold . . .

As long as a civilization is living, it is impossible to separate it from the people from which it arises, to such a degree is its wellspring concealed in their concrete behavior.

---

1 Johann Joachim Winckelmann (1717–1768), a forerunner of archaeology and one of the first to classify Greek art into periods. See his important work *The History of Art in Antiquity*, 1764, where he defines the goal of art as beauty. Footnotes provided by the translator except where noted.
2 In "The Greek State" (1871), a preface to an unwritten book, Nietzsche stresses the barbarism of the Greek state, with political passions raging, the necessity of slavery to make art possible, and the undignified nature of any kind of work, including art.

We must add that this metaphor of a spring is inadequate: it is not a matter of man on the one hand and his civilization on the other. Here a spatial image is a deformation. We should rather evoke the image of the soul, the principle of life, and the organs of the body which it animates. Just as an organic body and a living body are identical, man himself and the civilization he is imbued with are one. Our civilization is we ourselves; it is a body of human beings organically bound to each other, whose reciprocal relations of every kind are exactly what constitute civilization. We can no more separate ourselves from it than we can remove the mutual, harmonious relations from the organs of our body.

Furthermore, that is why the phenomenon of civilization is strictly undefinable: it is not outside of us as an object we might take hold of; just as with our individual lives, it is intermingled with us in a profound way. In fact, no one perceives the presence of the living civilization which surrounds him: whatever his social position or rank, it is as imperceptible as the air we breathe, or, better yet, as the health we have, whatever our build and strength. It is the same with everything else present in our lives, which we do not become detached from until we ourselves are overtaken by death, as a flower wilts when its stem is uprooted. A living civilization grows in silence through the synergy of all of its components. It is the same as with love or faith, the intensity of which is not expressed in a single act of awareness, since consciousness is already fully imbued with it: true lovers do not speak of their love, and are not the ones who say, "Lord, Lord, who will enter the Kingdom of the Father?"

Civilization, so difficult to grasp that we can only do it through images which suggest rather than reveal it, is just the same an act of human self-expression: it is in fact the standard expression of man, his visible projection, and in a way, his manner of life, onto the scene of history. It is the result of a certain mysterious force which leads him to rise above himself and to go beyond the level where all other living things in nature are fixed as soon as they appear in the world. While at its birth an animal is wholly an animal, endowed with an ensemble of instincts, reflexes, and automatic reactions which are deployed with an almost perfect spontaneity, power, and sureness, man only attains to what is appropriately called human existence through ever renewed labor. Man is, just as an animal, a *being belonging to the world*, but while an animal adapts immediately to the environment around it, man reacts to the world by building a civilization. Without civilization, man would be incapable of understanding the world, of becoming integrated into it, of establishing with it a relationship indispensable to his existence: he would be *without a world*, lost in a hostile universe which would reduce him to the state of an imperfect animal, out of joint, whom it would eject from its bosom. The feeling of anguish which seizes man during epochs when the civilization he has built is threatened with ruin has no other origin than the vague fear of death. Similarly, the rigidification of certain civilizations in decline signifies that man unconsciously surrounds himself with protective armor as inflexible and fossilized as possible in order to defer the inevitable eviction of people of his kind from the world scene.

To the extent that we can determine the essence of civilization, it seems that it is the exteriorization, often very complex, of man's reaction to the reality in which he must live. Its character is the collective equivalent of the character of an individual. Just as character is the expression of man's personal reaction to the presence of the world, beings, things, and events, civilization is the expression of his *fundamental* attitude towards reality, apprehended at a deep level, which the individual is always unaware of. This is without doubt the reason why the genius that brings together and condenses the elements of a mode of civilization appears paradoxically as the summit of an impersonal personality; the "I" clothed with its own character – sometimes suspect – abdicates here before the expression of a relationship of man with the world, brought forth from the depths of the inexpressible where each of us finds himself. It is moreover indisputable that all the great civilizations of the past have been metaphysical and contemplative, where the *sui generis* relationship of man to the universe is expressed through its essential functions which make it transparent: art, philosophy, religion, powerfully articulated together. It suffices to look back to the civilizations of China, India, Egypt, Greece, and the European Middle Ages.

THE AXIS OF A CIVILIZATION

It is obvious that these observations are only an approximation, where shadows filter in, elucidating some things rather than giving a complete explanation. Moreover, a living civilization – and even a dead civilization, in the measure to which we try to bring its soul back to life – is ceaselessly mysterious, shedding more light on us than we can project on to it. Yet the specific structure of a civilization permits us to discover its principal axis. If civilization shapes us more than we shape it, if it constitutes, according to a famous expression, a state where we receive more than we can give back by the personal work of each one of us, it is because it only weakly depends on our clear-sightedness and the rational goals we set. In fact, man works, suffers, and sometimes dies to build up a civilization, but the result of his efforts is less the work of his spirit and will than of the necessities of being and living, which are always with him. Thrust into the world by his birth, it is the relationship of his being with the world which demands of him that mode of expression which we call civilization. In this sense, civilization is a phenomenon as natural as the growth of a tree or the development of an animal. The action of the world around him on his being invincibly tends, like every action, to reveal and express itself. One could say in this regard that civilization is creative receptivity par excellence: it captures messages from the world, not like a mechanism set up by man, but as a living organism, and through the creative power of its vitality confers on them a human meaning and content: it brings to man the essence of the world in distilled form. It is not astonishing, then, that a nascent civilization is very near to the most immediate and sense-oriented aspects of the world. Through his sensations, man is rooted directly to the universe, and the civilization in which he expresses himself at this stage has something akin to the vague, amorphous mystery associated with this powerful receptivity of the senses, illuminated at times by flashes of lightning, as the vestiges of prehistoric art show us.

Now expression and impression are correlative. The potential of a gift is equivalent to the receptive potential of the recipient, and the more man opens up his soul to the presence of the world – to his neighbor, nature, beauty, God, the thousand and one secrets murmured by creatures – the more apt he is to give expression to them, in whatever manner, just as they are. He who is closed in on himself, on the contrary, will only draw from within an emanation of himself that superimposes itself on the real, masking it or suffocating it. Here everyday language is very significant. We say of a word, picture, song, silent moment, or look that it is expressive, not simply that it reveals a state of mind, but that it unmasks an actual manifestation of something real, and communicates the relationship which the mind has formed with it. These modes of expression "say something" to the degree that they have perceived "something", and this expressive function is only fully creative when it is filled with the actual presence of what it has perceived. So it is with the type of expression we call civilization: it creates because it receives; it blossoms and bears fruit because it has thrust its roots into the world and drawn up its nourishing sap. These two movements are but one and, far from being opposed to each other, like height and depth, they are complementary, participating in the same vertical movement.

In the world whose relationship with man is expressed and made human by civilization, man himself stands out, united to his kind through physical relationships, bonds of blood and kinship which he has formed as coming out of nowhere and which are imposed on him with the irresistible force of an obvious fact, arising from nature. It is not the mind, reason, or deliberate willing that engender these bonds, but life and its innate desire to grow. The relationship among men in the bosom of the family, first in the order of time, precedes the relationship of man to the world, and is written in the flesh of man, making him completely what he is. It is not the product of art, technical skill, or industry, but is like water gushing forth from the very source of life, thrusting man into existence, body and soul, with all his concrete characteristics, with his fellow man before him in a *primary* relationship which comes before all the others, save that which binds him to the very principle of being. All civilizations have their beginning in this initial relationship, enwreathed in a halo of religious origin. Nascent civilizations everywhere are linked to a social grouping, meaning an organic community of kinfolk (family, clan, tribe, *genos*, *gens*)[3] and to a cult of the divine. It is not by chance that the word *civilization* derives from *civis*, citizen, belonging to a city, whose familial and sacred character is known from the work of Fustel de Coulanges[4] and whose ancient designation, *policie* or *police* — today systematically debased into terms associated with surveillance and coercion — evokes the social and religious framework of the Greek *Polis*. It is the same with related words: *policé*, *urbanité*[5], which have now disappeared from everyday language. This historical

---

3   *Genos*, Greek for family or kin; *gens*, French for people.
4   1830–1889, French historian, author of *The Ancient City*, 1864.
5   Literary terms for, respectively, "highly civilized" and "urbanity."

and semantic phenomenon signifies the fact that civilization expresses an inborn relationship which man can neither control or dominate in any way because it is the foundation of the existence bestowed on him. That is why man, be he Greek or barbarian, is to some degree a civilized being: the pure savage, free from every relationship, which Rousseau dreamed of and which ceaselessly haunts the souls of our contemporaries, is either a myth or a monster. If it is true, as Hölderlin[6] says, that "birth is in large part decisive", the origin of civilizations constitutes a crucial witness to their nature: it means that civilization is the expression of human life, in the sense of the experience of a living relationship which man is incapable of transcending except by subterfuge, by deforming his nature as a being who is either civilized or on the path to civilization. Man can only overstep birth-imposed limits in an *imaginary* way, by splitting himself in two; one part, willfully scorned, derives from his origin and stagnates, and the other part, deliberately constructed by the mind, orients his action towards a world which is only material, to be transformed according to its schema. In other words, man can always deny his birth by transcending the fundamental relationship that restrains him, but he is then compelled to construct for himself an imaginary civilization which is only a form of expression devoid of content and life.

The life-serving nature of civilization, which continually nourishes its growth from the beginnings of its existence, is inaccessible to the mind: it can only be conceptualized when it is first lived. The fundamental relationship of man with the world precedes human knowledge and will; their role is limited to affirming it and participating in it by means of contemplation and action, or to denying it while creating mere images of authentic being and projecting them onto a bloodless and diminished life.

---

6   1770-1843, German poet and philosopher. The quote is from his poem "The Rhine."

All later development of civilization in its highest spiritual forms is based on an ever-deeper integration into its original life, whose inexhaustible archetype it is striving to express: where a civilization grows, one can discern the social and religious energy that fosters its development and permeates its most noble achievements. It is enough to recall the past.

As murky and troublesome to the intellect as this identity between civilization and the expression of life at its origins may be, it does not cease to shed light on the singular phenomenon of the polymorphism of civilizations known by man. In *A Study of History* Arnold Toynbee[7] points out that history has seen the birth of twenty-three different types of civilization, of which only five endure today, for the most part gravely limited in carrying out their vital functions. Why, then, are there civilizations in the plural, and not just one Civilization producing a unique, universal type of man? Why are the increasing arrogance of a civilization and its territorial expansion always a sign of degeneration? The witness of history is convincing: for a civilization the call to universality is the call to death. These two related phenomena have no other cause than the contrast if not antimony between the expression of life and life itself, which is always setting them in opposition to each other despite their complementarity. Understood in its substance, life is incommensurate to the expression of it, because it is overflowing, and its expression requires a form with limiting contours. On its own, life continually aspires to break through the concepts of time and space, and, according to the expression of Bergson, to overthrow death.[8] Life is necessarily lived and

7   (1889-1975), a ten-volume work tracing the development and decay of major civilizations.
8   Henri Bergson, 1859-1941, an important and influential French philosopher, Nobel laureate for literature, 1927. He upheld the primacy of a spiritual principle in the development of all life, and the continued existence of the human soul after death. See, for example, *L'énergie spirituelle*, 1919.

experienced within structures imposed by space and time, which shape it, as everyday experience as well as the fables of antiquity show. Beyond a certain point of growth and maturity, every living form deteriorates. Thus all living forms have their limitations and consequently take many different forms, differentiated by their relative, incomplete perfections. Only the Being who is life, expressing Himself through life itself, and who is the Word of life, triumphs over space and time. The expression of the fundamental relationship of man with the world necessarily constricts its breadth, and its very limitations give rise to various forms (and expressions). The activities which communicate this relationship take place in time and are submitted, like all activity, to the rhythm of birth and decline. Moreover, life is of an overflowing abundance, and if civilization is healthy, enabling man to live in the world, it should in turn be fully alive, variegated, multifaceted.

This is why, then, there is not nor can there be a *Christian civilization*, in the proper sense of the word, in spite of the abuse of this expression. Christian faith is independent of the civilization which it is raised up on. The proof is given to us by history and geography: Christianity failed to save decadent Roman civilization, and adapted itself to the new barbarian civilization which was going to lead to the Middle Ages; if it had fulfilled its universal mission, neither India nor China would have the same civilization as Europe. However, we have the invincible inclination to confuse our current civilization, born in Europe, and Christianity, not only because of a vague remembrance of the Middle Ages, where the leaven of the faith influenced the Western *Respublica Christiana*, but above all because modern civilization in decline, which engulfs us, in a confused way parasitically lives off Christianity, from whence it expects salvation, without adopting its requirements, and because Christianity for its part fears the collapse of its old framework, now worm-eaten.

ON THE DEATH OF A CIVILIZATION

CIVILIZATION AND LIFE

Since civilization is a form of life for man, like all life it has its vicissitudes, its rhythm, its uneven, meandering path. It would be vain to seek to discover, in any living civilization, a consistency, a linear development, or better yet what the modern spirit calls "unlimited progress." A civilization does not develop according to a rigorous sequence of theorems nor a dialectic of ideas. The essential virtue of life is its unpredictable capacity for renewal and inventiveness, and its unexpected nobility. This virtue dissipates if the soul of the civilization does not hold onto it.

From this point of view, the duality between the expression of a vital relationship and the relationship itself constitutes the weakness of every civilization, and, in the same measure, its strength. Its form and expression are a storehouse of latent yet powerful life: sources of vitality which accumulate; they lie seemingly dormant, growing in strength until little by little they achieve perfection. Seen as a whole, a civilization appears as a tradition which at a certain moment reaches the peak of its ascent, when the relationship between man and the world finds its eminent, sometimes unprecedented, expression. Without this long continuity over time, without tradition, civilization would never arrive at a human expression of the world. A civilization that despises tradition loses the vital reserves which make renewal and restoration possible, as well as its ability to mature while on the ascendant, following a path which, when looked at closely, twists and turns. The unifying consistency of a living civilization binds successive generations together, facilitates intuitive insight into the world among people who are able to understand each other across time and space, and cements their relationship with each other, opening the way to mature expression of this relationship.

Here everything depends on the relative spiritual and intellectual vitality of human beings and their ability to become integrated into the world. Why is this? There is no response to such a question, we must acknowledge: this is the essence of the mystery of civilization and of the individual. Just as there are people whose great vitality, brilliance, and genius are in harmony with life itself and others who are morally backward, retrograde, without influence on the world around them, so there exist civilizations full of life-giving sap and those that are stagnant. There is actually a lack of equality in the laws governing life and being: a certain tree in a forest grows taller than the tree next to it, which is rooted in the same soil; a certain civilization is on a higher level than others in the measure that the roots of those who create it penetrate more deeply into the experience of what is real. Life does not spread its riches abroad according to a set plan. In one case, tradition stemming from the inner essence of a civilization and the continuity of its expression are like the endurance of someone with robust health, with no awareness of how this is accomplished, with an alternating rhythm of activity and rest, an aptitude for accomplishing things, and moments of lively creativity. Another civilization will be characterized by routine, mechanical repetition in an unchanging pattern, maintained in a precarious existence by an ever-diminishing vitality. It is thus appropriate to distinguish between monotonous repetition, which is an indication of inner exhaustion (dead wood repeats itself, Péguy said)9 and a form of tradition that sows seed which always germinates fruitfully, season after season.

In the living, unified expression which is observed in authentic civilizations, different types of persons participate in it. Here again the analogies with nature are striking. The leaves of a tree are not identical; they only resemble

9   Some words to this effect are expressed in Péguy's *Note conjointe sur M. Descartes et la philosophie* cartésienne, 1914, meaning that a dead mind is like dead wood, stultified. Charles Péguy (1873–1914) was a French religious poet and essayist, whose work encompassed politics and social criticism. He died in action during World War I.

each other. No two are identical in the manner of two geometrical shapes of the same dimensions or two manufactured objects cast in the same mold. The differences among leaves, flowers, fruit, branches, trunk, and roots are still more obvious. All the parts of a tree, however, form one organic unity. All are interdependent and act in synergy as one form of plant life.

The distinctive characteristic of a true civilization is to bring together, *organically*, with unity in diversity, persons who without it would live as isolated individuals. The higher the level of a civilization, the more we see that its social, political, religious, aesthetic, and moral functions vary as their interrelationship grows stronger, and the more we observe that those who participate in these activities are not of equal merit, yet have joined forces in the same project. Again we see that the lived relationship of man with the world is not the same among individuals, but is, rather, symphonic, because life and its expression are differentiated everywhere: the fundamental relationship is multiplied with a kind of natural prodigality in other relationships with different, though unified, components, exactly like the seed of a tree or the embryo of a higher organism.

No matter which way we look, civilization appears as an abundance of relationships which themselves spring from an earlier relationship, itself extraordinarily mysterious, which is experienced in an unconscious way and rises to the level of *lived experience*. The civilized person moves about at his ease in the world characterized by his type of civilization, and, if transplanted to another domain, experiences a sharp pang of disassociation: a certain harmony, imperceptible to him before, has now dissipated. From now on he is alone, a stranger. A remarkable intuition of this situation led the Greeks to designate as *barbaroi* all those who did not share their lived experience of the world.

THE CYCLE OF CIVILIZATION

Well-being, feeling at ease, effortless achievement – which does not exclude work, an integral part of all attempts to express oneself – that is what characterizes the attitude of man in the arena of civilization: the human being finds himself in a world which corresponds to his inner vitality, that is, he is *within* a world that he *recognizes* in the forms developed according to his type of life; he coexists with his family members, who express themselves in communicating with him. He finds everything clothed with a familiar, friendly, neighborly character; the anguish of being alone is foreign to him. Through all the ups and downs of personal and collective life which are the lot of humanity, he always has *something to hold onto*; as harsh or destitute as his existence may be, it has a meaning. What is it? Most of the time he knows little or nothing about it. Yet he feels, experiences, and lives this meaning, which appears to him as connected to a reality beyond him yet part of his make-up, which he tries to put into words – because every life finds expression as a person moves and acts in the world – and that he finally identifies as his civilization, more or less multifaceted. This civilization in turn orients his action towards an end that he senses, and so on in an endless cycle. All modes of being and acting, from the humblest skill to the rites of many primitive religions, undergo this twofold pull. The expressions of man's inmost being come from his lived experience, and return back to him in a circular fashion; this reinforces the hold that the world has on his life and his corresponding desire to understand it. The mind of man is caught up in this back-and-forth rhythm of civilization.

Such is the brilliant apex of a civilization. Yet every life is destined for death: "We modern civilizations have recognized that we are mortal like the others."[10] Well before

---

10   Paul Valéry, *La crise de l'esprit*, 1914. Valéry, 1871–1945, was a French poet, philosopher, essayist, and considered to be the last of the symbolist poets

Paul Valéry, a disillusioned witness, man vaguely sensed this. This is why civilizations with a higher level of life give out their brightest lights, the most brilliant of all, before entering a long period of decline foretelling their definitive collapse. So it is with all forms of life: at the moment of maturity, the briefest period of time in the existence of a civilization or being, energies are mustered for one last blossoming. What is referred to as the Age of Pericles[11] or of Augustus[12]—a recognition of names that seem eternal—was in fact a period of a few years, the last moment in a civilization's resistance to death, when life triumphs, bursting forth in an unforeseen way, soon followed by the first signs of exhaustion.

This crucial phenomenon in the decline of civilizations sheds remarkable light on their nature, in the manner of an illness which reveals what good health actually is. As long as the lived experience of man in relation to the world unrestrainedly penetrates and envelops his various modes of self-expression, a civilization is sustained and prospers: life nourishes it without contributing to its exhaustion. Its form always constitutes a protective fortress for reality, because what is real continually tries to go beyond its limits. An unbroken continuity is established between different aspects of human existence and their fundamental relationship with civilization. Mutual influences and exchanges strengthen art, philosophy, and religion, shedding light on the situation of man in the world, and enriching these forms of expression. As long as these relationships exist, nothing in them rings hollow.

How is a fissure in civilization brought about? How does the form of a civilization slough off these relationships, empty itself of its substance, and transform itself

---

11   c.490–429 BC, leader of the government of Athens for thirty years, a period of prosperity and flourishing of the arts. The Age of Pericles represents all that was highest in Greek art and science.
12   63 BC–14 AD, first Roman emperor. The Augustan Age was the golden age of Roman literature and architecture.

into a mold which shapes a reality diminished by a kind of automatism? This degradation of a living force into something mechanical, a phenomenon simultaneously brought to light by the genius of both the peasant Péguy and the intellectual Bergson, is a very simple process, as shown by our own experience. It is rather surprising that this process has not been described more often, since it is so obvious. Perhaps we need to look at the tenacious influence of our delusion which masks the presence of death and which always characterizes the last years of a civilization.

The lived experience of a fundamental relationship, we have said, finds expression; this is, along with the existing level of vitality, the whole of a civilization. Now precisely because the relationship of man to the world is a lived experience, it totally permeates man in his entirety and affects his environment: man lives and expresses, in concentrated fashion, his relationship with everything affecting him intimately, his relatives and friends, the earth, the mysterious presence of the divine intermingled with nature. In this regard, the first civilizations were patriarchal, agricultural, and religious. Against this backdrop new civilizations with metal-working abilities appear, causing those which preceded them to weaken and disappear, as is seen in tottering civilizations in times of crisis. The highest forms of civilization even at this stage are those immersed in an experience of being that leaves behind a *permanent surplus* of vitality; as it is still present everywhere it transcends man, giving him the constant feeling of belonging organically to what is real. The soul, intelligence, will, and imagination, whose activity ceaselessly creates modes of self-expression, are in solidarity with life, which gives them their undefinable, concrete participation in existence. They closely depend on an inner, radiant warmth which is the very mark of every lived experience, stimulating their development and making them authentic. The more they open themselves to life, the more life is incarnated in them, and is shaped by their influence. A developing civilization thus expands from within to outside itself, with no rupture in the continuity between the real, man, and the expression of their relationship, as happens with every species of life. Civilization is ruled by the essential rhythm of every existence, which is its participation in life and subordination to its law of organic relationships, with their give and take.

Then a fissure introduces itself: all the expressions of the fundamental relationship, whatever they may be, can, even as *expressions*, become detached from man, like a dead leaf falling from a tree. These expressions take numerous forms: languages; use of colors, figures, and numbers; law; codes of behavior; rites; social conventions . . . which act as the intermediaries between man and the world, and through which passes a current of life, with the fundamental relationship now visible and palpable. So it is with the words we use in social relations and poems. Over all these forms of expression the threat of mechanization presses, insulating them within themselves, interrupting the ebb and flow of life, so that the mind which creates and orders them refuses to bow before the primacy of that relationship which it neither created nor ordered and which imposes itself on it. In other words, the negation of religion in all domains triggers automatism. The soul withdraws, along with its creations, to outside the network of relationships where the human being normally moves about. An inevitable consequence follows: the forms of civilization no longer share in human life, and man himself, instead of seeing himself as a center of communication, a node in exchanges with others, is transformed into a malleable material, ready to be molded into something devoid of life. Civilization is then replaced by a technique for dominating the world, where man, cut off from all his ties, considers himself as having transcendence over the world. The degeneration of the civilization is not long in coming, in the measure to which human vitality, coming up against artificial forms of expression which make it sterile, finds less and less of an opening to express itself. Then, equipped with lifeless forms of expression, man shapes, grinds down, homogenizes, and desperately mechanizes all of existence, including his own life, just to survive.

Moreover, we see ages in history when civilization penetrated man to his roots, like a soul, and others when it pressed down on him like a lead weight. At times it becomes integrated with the very being of man, from which it emerges and blossoms, infused in him like a rising sap which springs up, unable to contain itself. At times it only gives a superficial order to human life, like a veneer covering man's forlorn life, which in a quasi-hypostatic act takes hold of his being, absorbing it. The former type of civilization, immanent in man, constitutes the framework of his existence. The latter type is detached from human beings, hovers over them, and directs them, like a malevolent Platonic idea. Let us think for a moment of the attitude of the Greek in the ages of Pericles and Alexander, or of the Roman during the prosperity of the Republic, or of the last centuries of the French empire, when man is integrated into the world by means of civilization. In the latter type of civilization he continually strives to escape outside the confines of the real, his vital energy diluted in the mechanization of the civilization which he has developed. Everything happens as if man, at certain times in his history, had the power to produce a civilization at one with himself, relating him to the world in a visible way, while at other times, exhausted, anemic, deprived of vitality and energy, he abandons himself to the drift of a civilization which, no longer irrigated from within by the active presence of the human, uproots him from the world.

CONSCIOUSNESS AND UNIVERSALITY

It is the phenomenon of the world as *absent* that creates an awareness of the crisis which is affecting civilization. This is an absolutely natural process, as we have said. Now every normal human activity that is interrupted or threatened with disappearing from the scene immediately produces a keen, lucid intuition of the fact that it is necessary. So it is with our basic physiological functions: we only become aware of our stomach when digestion becomes sluggish. It is the same with the organic integration of man into the world which civilization creates. We are struck by the drama raging within civilization as it becomes more and more unhinged, when man, whom civilization has benefited, loses his roots. The mysterious elements which bind man to a world where religion has meaning, enabling him to give it a human character, fade away, to the benefit of a "new awakening". These elements are transferred from the arena of his life as a whole to the arena of his mind, from what he has experienced to what he has thought, truncating the conceptual from the rest of his life. In a final burst of activity, the mind tries to fill up the gaps it has left behind, hastily concocting replacements. Today we are so jaded that only some new ersatz substitute seems original to us. We have become insensitive to the artificial ambience where we make a show of living.

The first visible sign, yet also the most unnoticed, of the decline of civilization is that we are aware that we have one. With the utter lucidity of the sick person who recognizes the nature of his illness, we follow its development. We perceive one after the other the functions of civilized life, customs, art, science, philosophy, politics, social life, and religion, affected by a relentless process leading to decadence. Our awareness of this process sharpens, awakened by the breaking up of these functions. Our minds open up in proportion to the emptiness that seizes us, dominating us, forcing on us what they have independently created, with nothing to stop the process. This gives us a secret joy: we know that something evil is present, splitting us in two, one part fading away and the other interpreting in light of its perceptions the most subtle deviations, with cunning control over them. Today we are able to organize what is disorganized with an all-encompassing perspective, similar to an architect's plans, bringing together scattered elements. That is all we are capable of. Our awareness of the unicity of our civilization grows as the civilization disintegrates; what holds it together operates only at the level of the *intellect*, aided by what it has at hand: an abundance of sterile language, insidious deceit, and brutal force. However, life in reality is calm, forthright, unarmed.

If it is true that an organization dies when its inner coherence disappears, modern civilization has reached this stage. Nietzsche would undoubtedly not write today, "I came to you, present-day man, I came to the land of culture . . . And what happened to me? In spite of my fear, I had to laugh. My eyes had never seen anything so motley! . . . With face and limbs painted fifty different ways: so you sat there to my great astonishment, present-day men! And with fifty mirrors around you, fifty mirrors which flattered your play of colors, repeating it! . . . And if one scrutinized the heart, whom would you convince that you have a heart? You seem to be formed out of colors and scraps of paper stuck together."[13] Civilization is no longer unity in diversity; it is no longer what it was in Nietzsche's time, pure diversity. By a huge mental effort, it has become an abstract, formal unity of a disjunctive multiplicity of identical beings, looking at itself in the unique mirror of "the human consciousness held to be the highest divinity."[14] We are immersed in a spatial-temporal

13 *Thus Spake Zarathustra*, No. 36, "The Land of Culture." Nietzsche's well-known book (1883–1885) is an imaginative philosophical narrative upholding freedom from any creed or philosophical system, indeed from any principles. In it he proclaimed the death of God.
14 A characteristic thought of Nietzsche.

continuum of thought which is reduced more and more to a single common *intellectual* denominator, and thus we live in a morbid discontinuity with the past. If we look at the great ideological currents that intervene in civilization and if we consider, rather than their various sources, the marshy delta into which they flow, we are dumbfounded by how alike they are in their poverty of thought. Marxism, capitalism, and a certain kind of Christianity vie with each other as they move towards the domination of the world by their modes of thought. This world, though, is just an abstract terrain, gray, uniform: we look in vain for the land where men of flesh and blood dwell. It is an algebraic expression with no personal encounters, where one's *fellow man* is not in sight, but has faded from the awareness of all humanity. In the aforementioned systems of thought, people are no longer related to each other by a certain *je ne sais quoi*, impossible to describe, which obliges them, in the course of a good many conflicts and tribulations, to join together in the warm atmosphere of small communities where each person effortlessly understands the other. Everything happens as though the different organs of the vast body of humanity, the brain, loins, heart, – but whom would you convince that you have a heart? – and the different kinds of cells had lost their protective walls and had been transformed into units very much the same, with nothing connecting them, placed next to each other by the cold presence – interrupted by bursts of "mysticism" – of the "spirit" dominating them. Civilization becomes just a matter of human atoms which it causes to disintegrate, and from which it hopes to draw out unknown psychic energy to renew the face of the earth under the direction of an intelligence, whether it be spiritual or material, political or economic, gnostic or scientific, matters little, since it is present, guiding poor, bleeding humanity towards its particular "good." Following each catastrophe, each progression in the abasement of concrete human values, civilization announces, through the mouths of its most qualified interpreters, that the "spirit" of justice, charity, and access to all earthly goods by means of an elaborate, hyperorganized technology unfailingly does its work in an atomized world. The more authentic life passes away, the more the mind conjures up a new form of life in a new, devitalized world.

This, then, is the drama of the workings of the mind at the time of profound crisis in a civilization: the fundamental relationship of man with the world only exists as an idea, a product of the imagination, given the real rarity of actual thought in the human species. Without the affinity between man and the world, characteristic of the past, the world no longer speaks silently to man in a thousand voices drifting into his unconscious and communicating its secrets; man does not respond with a corresponding silent affection. He becomes much less aware of his place in the universe, which makes man and the world mutually incommunicable, without any sense of fraternity. Through his mode of perception, which colors with greater or lesser clarity his awareness of the ends of civilization, *man admits he is incapable of participating in the real world and of working with others organically in a specific community*: he flees from everything that is, he flees from his very being in order to focus on the idea or image he has fashioned of himself and of reality. He substitutes a relationship he has dreamed up for a living relationship. The religious in his cell who discourses on marriage, conjugal relations, systemic reforms, without the least concrete experience, the politician who reorders society, the scientist in his laboratory who outlines plans for the city of the future, the engineer who treats man like a machine, the artist who works according to his own theory of art, all of us, having in mind a preconceived idea of one or another aspect of life, are borne away by a current of thought that, in a manner insidious or brutal, prevents us from being ourselves. Most people today prove themselves incapable of living *their own* life: a dying civilization marks out innumerable escape routes. The man of today takes refuge in an abstraction, seated in his intelligence, resulting from his rupture with the nuptial pact between civilization and nature, which had integrated him into a world adapted to his measure and his capacity to embody what is spiritual.

The second sign marking the end of every civilization in decline is the tendency to impose itself on the world: this phenomenon, transcending space and time, is always and everywhere the same. Capitalism, Marxism, and Christianity, which all have a share in the *orbis terrarum*, [15] are already moderating their factitious differences in many areas, and, finding each other vaguely agreeable, are getting ready for a kind of cosmic fusion effected by a single high-tension current of "collective spirituality". No doubt these systems and doctrines are still in violent conflict with each other, just as there is no doubt that through the voices of the guarantors of orthodoxy, Christianity denies condoning ideas condemned by the faith, yet the moralist who ponders the customs and mentality of people today cannot help but note among both the elite and masses a distinct syncretistic tendency. Inasmuch as Christianity becomes detached from itself and is no more than a religious exaltation similar to that attained by various kinds of theosophy, or a superficial code of conduct whose influence does not penetrate beyond the brain, it does not escape the irresistible fascination of the disembodied forms of contemporary consciousness. In short, within humanity a global affinity for this consciousness and a change in perspective are experienced, through a more intense awareness of its worldwide ascendancy: in a gigantic melting pot every distinction among men is being obliterated.

These two indications are indisputably found in ancient civilization in its death pangs. Every civilization that abandons the fundamental relationship, *always concrete*, of man

---

15   A Latin expression meaning "world."

to the world, to revel in the prestige of an abstract idea, is marked with the seal of death. Every civilization that extends throughout the world and goes beyond the limits required by the expression, always well-defined and limited in scope, of its life and appropriate cultural exchanges, abandons its roots and loses its depth.

But what differentiates modern consciousness and global aspirations from those of antiquity is their oppressiveness and, dare it be said, their power, never before seen, to create a uniform type of human being. Contemporary man fashions an exceptional image of himself and transforms it into reality, in a cycle which originates in man and returns to man, bypassing the demands required by full participation in life. Man becomes transcendent to himself, paying the price for this effort: the suppression of an organic diversity, the deification of the great beast of Plato, [16] the leveling of the differences in individual personalities to create a global collective consciousness, deprived of true life and thought. For the relationship between man and the world cannot be conceived and lived out by a collectivity: it is the prerogative of each person. My organic relationship with my family, my social community, with all the forms of culture which give expression to these relationships, is uncompromisingly personal: another person is incapable of grasping this, experiencing it, understanding it, except from without, and in only an abstract way. No one can take my place in the world, no one is interchangeable with me, unless we are all reduced to the condition of robots. While one may now refer to this situation as "the end of the conflict between man and nature," as Marx does, "the mastery of the earth through technology," with private or state capitalism, the "primacy of spirit over matter," according to the ambiguous expression of an emasculated

---

16   In Plato's *Republic* he likens human desires and instincts to a great beast, seated in the stomach and dominant in the masses, in comparison with intelligence and courage, seated respectively in the head and heart.

Christianity fascinated by the myth of a new earthly paradise, these are merely verbal distinctions. They intersect with each other and become identical on one actual point: man is the measure of the "world" he has created; man constructs a civilization which as he comes under its laws no longer functions to situate him in reality; like a demigod, he works the smooth, soft material which henceforth represents being for him, and impresses on it his own image, lusterless, deified. Our contemporaries are in the grip of the strangest of idolatries, civilization. While civilization dies of inner wasting, adversaries, outwardly fighting each other, reconcile spontaneously around an effigy representing them, offered to the whole world, for its "defense", "salvation", "advancement" and "purification" . . . Like the doctors in Molière, [17] adversaries disagree about needed methods, remedies, and purgatives, yet they all hope for a revival. That is the tragicomedy of today.

Abstract and universal, modern civilization presents one final characteristic: it is no longer the expression of a participatory relationship which man has with the world, it is only an expression *apart from him*, developing according to its own rules, without reference to concrete men, working against any final traces of an organic relationship that it encounters, putting itself above geographical limitations and past experience.

Hence the following subsidiary observations, often noticed but seldom connected to their originating principle. First, "civilization", to achieve its ends, must reduce the old world to dust, silence the impotent voices that come from the hearts of many living beings, and effect a radical transformation of values. It causes traditional structures, which have emerged little by little from the very substance of man in the course of millenia, to wither away and crumble, in order to center the world on itself and increase its impact

---

17   1622-1673, major French dramatist who satirizes doctors in several of his comedies. Vain and incompetent, they never cure anyone.

on those living in it. Civilization no longer recognizes men, things, or local landscapes that imbued past cultures with their mysterious transparency, when in the past it penetrated to the heart of their mutual coexistence. The "civilization" of uprooted man advances everywhere through forced entry in order to break up the world. It is not by chance that apparently disparate elements join together today in a common determination to dismantle the components of the world and of man in order to put them back together in a lifeless, mechanized environment. We mention the hodgepodge of psychoanalysis; divorce; cohabitation; popular and elitist art, which specialize in producing a shock to the nervous system and other visceral reactions; the intrusion of politics into every nook and cranny of life, particularly in the workplace; aggressive mass propaganda; sprawling cities where each resident lives in an airtight cell; the singular role of agitators; the positions taken by newspapers, aggressive to the point of psychosis; the disjunctive effect on communal life of participation in meetings, large demonstrations, and occasional gatherings in public places, with social groups easily dissolved and then formed anew; the effect of movies, advertising, glaring lighting, and noise; the utmost ease in getting from one place to another, which takes our attention away from people and things; the constant chaos issuing from the radio; the tearing apart of society caused by the disruption of wars; the dreadful euphemism *displaced persons*; [18] individual and collective gangsterism; the social experiments conducted on man *in vivo*; the widespread cult of hate; and to bring the list to an end, for the time being, nuclear fission and its consequences. With such an increasingly common scenario, which includes even the countryside, mountains, forests, and sea, where the contact of man with nature becomes a prostitution of the latter to the former, where few distinctions are made between one thing and another, where people and things,

---

18   In English in original.

without a lasting relationship, are placed next to each other with no coexistence in time or space, undermined in their very foundation, dissolving little by little into a vast lifeless stream, dreadfully bleak, made up of a succession of disjointed moments.

On the other hand, we must admit that civilization's conquest of all available territory stems from the desire, haunting and driving it, to free itself from restrictions imposed by local conditions, such as the climate, and the presence of other civilizations scattered around the planet. As colonization shows all too well, modern civilization does not adapt well to the other forms of civilization it encounters; it does not establish any kind of cultural exchange, such as Spain attempted in her overseas empire. Modern civilization imposes itself with no consideration for the milieus where it inserts itself, as though like a pure spirit it scorned other modes of earthly existence. No geographic obstacle stops it. As it spreads, it engulfs what it finds, but puts down no roots, something it cannot do. It forms a stratum encompassing latitudes and longitudes, devouring, like a vampire, all organic resources still extant here and there. It transcends geography, in keeping with its nature, in order to absorb countries, races, and souls into a sort of mechanical world soul. It erases the effects of time as well. It is not necessary to dwell on its scorn for the essential element in all living civilizations: tradition. It has no memory, consigning to oblivion the experience of centuries and even those of the recent past in its characteristic forgetfulness. It lives in the present moment while squandering the future.

Thus modern civilization extends its new order outside of the normal experience of time which makes the hearts of men beat in unison. Face to face with a world and humanity whose reciprocal affinities have now dried up—they are invariably reestablished in the secrecy of history to form another civilization—modern civilization nonetheless undertakes an unprecedented initiative: to bring together the world and the peoples scattered all over it, to a greater and greater degree as its geographic reach is extended, without any concern for renewing anywhere the concrete affective bonds which formerly held people together. It needs to find a common denominator as vague and devoid of content as possible, capable of bringing together this chaotic multiplicity and forming little by little, from the top on down, the molds of various sizes which will shape people and confer a sense of cohesiveness. Work of a "spirit" imposing its schemas on a humanity without substance, it spreads everywhere through deceit. No longer do man and the world work together in a mutual interaction from which issue social, economic, political, aesthetic, and religious structures as befits their development. The man who has permitted his roots to rot and his ability to perceive the concrete things in the world to deteriorate is then doomed to "organize" the world beyond the constraints of time, starting with abstract theories and plans, themselves situated outside time. He faces a world which has lost its human countenance.

This is where modern civilization finds its common denominator: in a world which is now only *matter*, and whose specific components, beauty, greatness, nobility, ontological depth, mystery, the reflection of God, have been effaced. For matter, as the most profound philosophies show, is by essence indeterminate, empty, undefined potentiality, with an aptitude for all representations: modern civilization, with its undefined form, could not but be attracted by matter; its "spirit" had to be materialist, as soon as it sought to delay its inevitable expulsion from the world scene, and proposed to all people an identification of their nature with its abstract, anonymous, inorganic universality. Matter, the object of all sorts of desires, and endowed with an infinite divisibility, lives up to its innate drive toward dissolution.

Thus we witness the most disconcerting paradox of the present situation: the relationship between man and the world is scarcely anything but material, while the human spirit, more and more factitious, demands of itself an increasing number of subterfuges, those of science and technology, endowed with ever more glory, which allow it to dominate and "organize" the chaos. The human mind unceasingly develops new social structures, on a world-wide scale today, hurling what it finds into volcanic dust to effect a new amalgamation. Always on the alert, the "spirit" of present civilization is driven to a redoubled vigilance. The least crack in the system results in collapse, as many wars and revolutions have ominously presaged. Without a realization of this, accessible to the initiated who rule over the "great beast", deprived of authentic life and thought, fulfilling the old dream of Mephistopheles: "one mind is enough for a thousand hands,"[19] without the princes of this world who, in spite of themselves, driven by the nature of events, set up their domination over the whole world, princes of finance or politics, next to whom the princes of art and science have but a secondary role, modern civilization would have already collapsed. Their realization of this is only the ultimate manifestation of their unbending stance.

Everything will begin anew as small groups of people with mutual love rebuild an earthly civilization under the gaze of God.

THAT WHICH IS HUMAN IS CYCLICAL

The breakdown of civilization, as long and painful as it may be, drives only cowardly, weak people to despair and violence. Civilizations are like generations lasting for centuries, and like them succeed each other, in the words of the poet, like leaves on trees. [20] Everything that is human is ruled by the principle *corruptio unius generatio alterius*, [21]

---

19 Mephistopheles, a devil in Goethe's *Faust*.
20 Unidentified reference.
21 Latin, the corruption of one is the birth of another.

of which the ancient wisdom of Greece and the East had a profound intuition. Everything in the natural world is subjected, *inasmuch as it belongs to nature*, to the rhythm of life and death, which succeed each other in imitation of eternity. And civilizations are natural phenomena.

The esoteric idea of the circle, which the West has unfortunately lost, is of utmost importance in understanding the fate of civilizations. We are so bewitched by the unconscious conviction that our civilization has escaped from this law, because it is the timeless work of deified reason, that we no longer even see the circular movement of nature, not to mention the world of astronomy. It is enough to recall the cycles of day and night, summer and winter, the ebb and flow of the tide, sleep and wakefulness, growth and decline, birth and death, and their endless repetition. Here we may add heredity, the circulation of blood, impulses of nerves, reflex reactions, the rhythm of walking, flying, swimming, dancing, recurring motifs in music, rhythms and refrains in poetry, rhythms which appear in all the arts, even the most static; also the continual return to the principles on which all living knowledge is based, the continuous alternation between unity and duality pulsating from surges of emotion, the universal belief in a world coming from God and returning to Him after innumerable vicissitudes. From Job, who cries out in his prayer, *"manus tuae fecerunt me et plasmaverint me totum in circuitu* [22] to Gérard de Nerval, "Time will restore the order of days of yore,"[23] including the Chinese yin and yang and the eternal return of the Greeks and Nietzsche,[24] every history of the natural world and of individual and collective man

---

22 Your hands have made me, and would you now turn round and destroy me? (Job 10:8).
23 From "Delfica" a poem evoking the cult of Apollo at Delphi and predicting the return of the gods of antiquity. Nerval (1808-1855) was a major French Romantic poet.
24 A concept formulated in ancient India, Egypt, and Greece holding that the universe and all existence has recurred and will continue to recur ad infinitum and taken up again by Nietzsche.

develops in a series of systoles and diastoles, themselves encompassed in more sweeping pulsations, and, in the end, in the basic cycle of life and its unfathomable mystery.

It is without a doubt possible for us to work out an objective theory of this cycle, in which we are included and from which we cannot remove ourselves, so as to put it in front of us just like an object; the cycle, however, is not an object, but life itself. Thus it escapes positivist science, which only considers a being in order to reduce it to elements deprived of any relationship between dualities, and when all is said and done, to nothingness, as Meyerson has shown. [25] In this regard, it is of great significance that science is incapable of directing its investigations, evaluating its discoveries, and interpreting its findings on nature other than in a linear fashion, its course of action following a straight, horizontal line. Some examples are its ideal of reducing everything to mathematics and its theories on evolution and on unlimited progress, which constitute its asymptotes; [26] science penetrates the essence of nature only superficially. The experiments contributing to it lack depth and only order being according to one dimension: the line which links antecedents and consequences of phenomena. The experience of life cannot be separated from time lived, which cannot be reduced to a quantity; it is always reconnecting with itself, forming a circle. Far from being rectilinear and orienting itself at all costs towards what is new, life centers on itself and perpetually finds that it is like unto itself: there is nothing new under the sun! A wisdom-directed life rediscovers itself while enriching itself, and enriches itself while rediscovering itself. Yet since it is

25 Emile Meyerson (1859-1933), Polish-French chemist and philosopher of science. He worked to refute the positivist bias in science, holding that science involves the effort to discover what is hidden from us, not just the ordering of data from observations; there is a tension between rationalizing thought and nature's resistance to a complete understanding of phenomena.

26 An asymptote is the line that a curve on a graph approximates as it approaches infinity.

a living thing, it has its limits, like all forms of life, and it acknowledges this: it comes up against an insuperable mystery everywhere. Having limits, it can and must die: that is the ultimate mystery where it attains to its destiny. This is why human wisdom, rich as it may be, is sadness: its substance is sorrow, and after suffering, death.

Science, on the contrary, boasts of a vision of triumph and joy: it progresses towards innovation in a straight line. But, as an inherent consequence, it says nothing to us: science is tangential to life, which in an obscure way requires more than this meager objective knowledge, beyond which science never advances because it is subjected to the rhythm of polarity, ending in death. No form of science can quench the thirst of man, unless he were to lose his desire for the springs of life.

Of course a living civilization, where wisdom is accumulated, is also drawn to death as to a magnet, only in order to be reborn, like wisdom itself, in a later incarnation. A civilization such as ours, which mimics scientific progress to escape its mortal destiny and to extend itself ad infinitum, does not break loose from this eternal norm, because it survives only by refusing to be living and to enable man to live. It is already a dead civilization before being swept away by the cyclical movement of history. Every living element in it prepares the future for another civilization. The varnish of its science covers over its barbarity, the upheavals of which cause its surface to crack.

It is thus necessary to be resigned to the death of modern civilization, from which we cannot remove ourselves as long as we are caught up in its workings. Like every preceding civilization, it will die. Nothing will save it, because its attempt to remove itself from the rhythm of life and death by technical and scientific stratagems only anticipates its integration into the cycle that affects everything human. Nothing will save it, not even Christianity. Let us not be deluded by false hope. Christianity only saves what is eternal in man, and the cycle of civilizations is only a faint image of eternity. Man escapes the cycle which rules over nature only through the supernatural, or utter despair: the circle opens up only from on high, or from below. At the end of our civilization, it is a matter of assuring the salvation of what cannot perish, of what most resembles the eternal: the fundamental relationship of man with creation, and, beyond this world, with the Creator, while being true to himself with all that this entails.

CHAPTER 1
The Conflict between Spirit and Life

S AINT-EXUPÉRY DESCRIBES CIVILIZA-
tion as "a heritage of beliefs, customs, and knowledge, slowly acquired over the course of centuries,
sometimes difficult to justify logically, but which are their
own justification, like roads, if they lead somewhere."[1]
Does present civilization lead anywhere? It seems apparent
that the world where we live is becoming more and more
inhuman, and that civilization is in the process of turning
against man. It is pointless to emphasize further this bitter
observation. But what does this mean? What aspect of it
surfaces in our consciousness?

A CIVILIZATION ABSTRACTED FROM LIFE

One could characterize present-day civilization like this:
we feel, to one degree or another, that the civilization that
surrounds us, intended to help us live, weighs on us, that
we with our whole being are no longer one with it, that
it is detached from us like a kind of carapace or covering,
continually threatening to suffocate us. The civilization
which should serve as a way of life for us is today a way
of suffering and death.

But this first observation is not yet sufficient. If civilization becomes more and more separate from our being
and daily life, becoming something outside of ourselves
working to form us from without, if we are sustained

---

1   *Pilote de guerre*, 1942. Saint-Exupéry (1900-1944), French, a commercial pilot, Air Force reconnaissance pilot during World War II, author of
memoirs, such as *Pilote de guerre*, and autobiographical fiction, including
the immensely popular *The Little Prince*.

in life by it less and less and suffer and die from it more and more, if in our concrete day-to-day life with its usual activities we find it burdensome and are no longer able to integrate it into our lives, then we must focus our research on the overall nature of present civilization and its detached, disembodied character, disconnected from our lives.

Now what does the isolated, what is not really lived, what is disembodied, consist of par excellence, if not the abstract? This opposition between the abstract and the concrete, between an idea and reality, is what drives the diagnosis of the crisis of civilization.

Humanity is in the process of succumbing to indigestion from a surfeit of ideas, noble or vile, Machiavellian or naive, which are all characterized by a kind of inability to become incarnate in life other than through violence or ruse; they are in disaccord with that deep, obscure instinct which, at the gravest moments of destiny, impels man to triumph over death. If we observe our contemporaries, even the most uncouth and simple-minded, for the most part they seem to us to be caught in a huge network of ideas which they themselves have either worked out, or received passively from the ambience, ideas deriving only from degraded cerebral activity, deaf to all calls to an authentic existence, ideas from which, very paradoxically, they expect salvation! People of today are trying to free themselves from their destiny, generating ideas which imprison them, chaining them to their fate in an ever more distressing manner. They are not attached to this or that concrete reality of daily life, or to this specific woman, for example, or to this type of work, this corner of the earth, but rather to sex, to a theoretical concept of work, to a political doctrine, all of which obscures and absorbs these manifestations of reality.

Let us look at the first point. As Bergson has said, current civilization, like every civilization which is falling apart, has an aphrodisiac character. [2]

---

2 *Les deux sources de la morale et de la religion*, Félix Alcan, ed., 1937.

Most of our contemporaries are attracted less by a certain specific woman than by any woman at all. That is not saying enough. Their stagnant idea of sex takes hold of whatever notion they come across, and eagerly draws life from this notion. All points of view are colored by a widespread artificial sexuality, but this sexuality is a mental construct rather than something springing from life. The proof of this is that the sexual response no longer has any biological purpose: on the one hand, it functions mechanically, like a receptacle that is alternately emptied and refilled; on the other hand it constantly has recourse to mental artifices. In these decadent people, the eternal feminine Goethe speaks of is no more than an abstract term. Look at the image of woman popularized in the movies, advertisements, and fashion: as physically unattractive as could be, artificial, the product of a sophisticated intellect corresponding to a disordered instinct always looking for more ways to express itself. Consider the vamp or pin-up: all their features appear lifeless. It is moreover significant that the unrestrained sexuality of our age is caused not by an excess of life justifying itself beyond measure, but by creations of the mind, images, the arduous labors of dress designers, make-up artists, hair stylists . . . A sexually healthy man has no need of these interventions.

We must insist on the place sexuality holds in modern civilization, not only because of its prominence, but because it is without doubt the most powerful of man's vital impulses (it bears the whole weight of human history) and disturbances in how it functions constitute an indispensable index of a profound change in a civilization's customs. The pan-sexuality rampant in contemporary culture, which paved the way towards a general conceptualization of history through the work of Freud, tends to detach itself more and more from concrete standards of behavior in order to hoist itself up to the level of abstraction.

The incursion of sexuality into the domain of the mind no doubt characterizes all times and places, as witnessed by the tragedies and comedies of humanity. It is here that the project of incarnating the mind in the body,[3] a moral blot in man, proves to be most intransigent. Even without overvaluing sex and the mind itself, the harmony between the two will always be precarious, doomed to failure: it is a matter of the union between what most pertains to the body and what most pertains to the mind in man! Sexual morals weaken and as it were get bogged down in mud when religion loses its vigor, resulting in their exaltation beyond proportion: the example of Greco-Roman morals after the collapse of ancestor worship and the current moral situation are sufficiently eloquent!

However, the aggressive nature of the sexual instinct can be understood in two ways, taking a twofold form, one healthy,[4] the other unhealthy, depending on the nature of antagonistic forces and the balance between them: either the sexual instinct is consistent with the trajectory of a dis-ordered vitality which breaks through the dikes of the mind, or it insinuates itself into the sponge-like terrain of an intelligence filled with gaps, which it saturates, transform-ing the underlying weakness of the mind into a swampy bog. The triumph of sexuality is thus not always a result of its power: it also derives from the insidious weakness and complicity of the intellect.

The first of these modes comes from an excess of vitality, of an unleashing of animal tendencies which are geared to the transmission of life – their end – and which, overpow-ering the intellect, seek to recover their purely biological function. This is the classical sin of the flesh where the mind intervenes only in a negative way, by failing to control the powerful instinctual responses acting independently of

---

3   De Corte here appears to be referring to the domination of the body by intellectual ideation.
4   That is, which does not proceed from a disordered intellect.

the mind, and in and of themselves healthy. Varende has portrayed a noteworthy example of this (now increasingly out-of-date) in *Nez de Cuir, gentilhomme d'amour*.[5] Neither the severest moralist nor the doctor most concerned with anomalous abnormalities would detect the slightest flaw in the instinctual foundation of an act, certainly sinful, where the biological function is in and of itself free from guilt. Since the exercise of the intellect, merely repressed in the midst of these powerful forces, remains intact, its working in conjunction with what is most animal in man, if this biological function is healthy, will always be possible. One could say that there is nothing unhealthy in La Varende's protagonist from a moral or medical perspective, since his intellect, if he consents to sin, is not implicated in the unleashing of his sexual powers so as to take pleasure in them. Since his intellect does not intervene in his life, it remains capable of becoming incarnate in it.[6]

The second form is quite otherwise, and the most widespread. The work of Miller[7] is an example. If the sexual instinct in a man fully alive is directed to its goal in a healthy manner because it is driven by its biological end, and because it has a tendency to operate as pure instinct – it is the most animal of our instincts, which gives it great potential to function independently, given a moral failure of the intellect – the same instinct in a devitalized man lacks the same intensity. He can only act with the aid of mental constructs which actively intervene.

---

5   Jean de La Varende (1887-1959), French writer whose work included novels, short stories, and biographies. In the novel referred to here, La Varende recounts the adventures of a notorious Don Juan. The conversion of the character at the end of the tale is consonant with De Corte's assertion that a disordered sexual life does not necessarily imply a disorder of the intellect.
6   Rather than countenancing sin, De Corte seems to be emphasizing here the fact that the intellect, not deformed by a false idea of sex, does not come into play in sexual sins of this type.
7   Henry Miller, 1891-1980, American novelist, some of whose works were banned for a time in the US due to explicit sexual content.

This is extremely grave: where sexual emotion has a role associated with the biological goal of sex, it remains capable of coming under the aegis of the intellect and being oriented to complete, perfect human love where both souls and bodies are united. But where an impoverished instinct requires mental stimuli to become active, the organic fusion of the intellect and the biological life force becomes impossible. When an individual's mental faculty weakens in a society characterized by an exuberant sense of life, it can turn towards concrete values otherwise beyond its reach, towards God, for example, and then be strengthened morally in order to become incarnate in life instead of being trampled by it. As soon as the life of a society becomes anemic, it lacks this resource: man's inner life, turned inward on itself and finding no support, degenerates and turns away from its project, befitting a human being, of becoming incarnate in what is real, only to base itself on the abstract. Unable to become grafted onto a life that is authentic, how could the mind have a connection with the concrete, with existence outside itself? *Nihil in intellectu quod non prius fuerit in sensu*,[8] an aphorism we must constantly repeat to ourselves. How could the mind be enriched by reality in the concrete if the bridges leading to it are tottering, full of cracks? The only resource left to it is to turn in on itself forever in the contemplation of itself and its ideas: setting in motion a merely superficial, automatic, form of thought, with its inevitable obsessions, scruples, and fears. One can then say that the weakening of the dynamic quality of life is always correlative to an artificial use of logic and the application of the mind to a series of mechanized abstractions: an impoverished awareness of the world is overcompensated by a false consciousness, the equivalent of counterfeit and devalued currency.

This is the resulting effect on modern man: an emasculated sexual emotion penetrates the intellect, from then

---

8   Latin, There is nothing in the mind that does not come from the senses.

on obsessed by the idea, in an almost Platonic sense, of sex. However, since man always tends toward unity of being until he becomes mad or dies, this abstract idea of sex compromises his life, weak and impotent, and overexcites him, as though whipping him, and masks his lack of strength. The detonation of the sexual instinct affecting the immense majority of our contemporaries requires a correct interpretation: it does not stem from an excess of vitality which liberates man; on the contrary, it derives from a lack of vitality which, passing through the distorting prism of the brain, distends the sexual instinct, inflating it like a balloon.

We find other quite clear examples of the same phenomenon in the situation of man with respect to the different natural communities in which he normally takes part, whether through birth, family, or vocation and type of work, or by virtue of his place in the history of his region or country. It is most remarkable that these social groupings have evolved, in parallel fashion, towards a state of abstraction which has nothing to do with actual life, other than exercising a destabilizing and corrosive influence over communities. The family is no longer an organic group of persons whose ends and interactions are analogous to those of the organs in a body: it has become a merely legal entity tending to have no other existence than what is accorded to it in civil registries. Trades, stricken in their cohesiveness by the Chapelier Law, [9] are swept into the orbit of an unbridled capitalist economy where the mathematical, abstract law of profit above all things holds sway, or into the orbit of a nationalist economy governed by a soulless bureaucracy. The fatherland becomes identified more and more with ideology pure and simple, which totally reshapes all its components.

We see before our eyes what is occurring in history, a vast transmutation of all values, from the concrete into the abstract, from lived existence into an automatized idea.

---

9   1791, annulled in 1884, banned workers' associations and strikes, thus promoting free enterprise.

39

Freed from all constraints and the necessities of concrete life, the machinery of an abstract idea is in the process of imposing itself on the inner being of man and refashioning him according to its schema. The trend of nationalistic and totalitarian doctrines, more threatening than ever in spite of their apparent defeat, is the tangible proof of the irony of a destiny which drags all men to their peril, even as they struggle to overcome it. We have entered a new era, where according to the prophecy of Hegel, the concept struggles against existence [10]: it seems that its triumph is now assured.

We could do research and discover in all sectors of contemporary life this slow, decisive absorption of the concrete by the abstract and of existence by an idea.

First of all, in art. It is sufficient to underline two well-known characteristics: art is becoming more and more cerebral and abstract; it is influenced more and more by ideological elements, especially political, foreign to its essence. Art living its own life and connected to the experiential is tending to disappear: the novel is being transformed into a treatise on sociology, poetry into an explanation of the unconscious; music, painting, and sculpture are becoming "a cerebral entertainment similar to a sufficiently difficult crossword puzzle" [11]; architecture incorporates engineering techniques to a greater and greater degree . . .

We could say as much about philosophy. Whether it is a matter of Marxism or a certain kind of existentialism, the purely formal devices of dialectics and sequences of concepts are replacing the lived experience of life. For the Marxist, the world is not an organic ensemble of multi-faceted persons, but a homogeneous economic substance where each particular manifestation of reality is diluted, merged into a kind of plastic, fluid mass, in perpetual

10   Here it seems that De Corte is referring to Hegel's system of dialectical thought, where thesis is followed successively by antithesis and synthesis, in a continually reiterated process. Reality is shaped by this dialectical process. See Hegel's *Science of Logic*, 1812–1816.
11   Unidentified quote.

motion, onto which the concept of socialism, by means of strictly materialist methods, comes to imprint a new face. Let us imagine for a moment about what this represents for the man-in-the-street Marxist, and the realities associated with his life. These realities no longer exist. Instead, abstractions have been projected onto existence; widespread ideas become one with man: the boss, banks, holdings, traitors bringing starvation . . . Other opposing ideas, just as abstract, only await the Great Day [12] to insert themselves into the stuff of existence and shape it as they see fit. The same observation, interpreted in the opposite way, holds for commonplace anti-Marxist. Similarly, for the emulators of Sartre existence has no consistency: it is weak, flaccid, mucky. Man only gives it a form through projects accomplished in his unlimited liberty. In this regard, existentialism represents perhaps the best and most decisive witness today's man can give of himself.

As for religion, its evolution is obvious. After turning into an abstract deism, where the existence of a concrete God makes way for a kind of impersonal law, a sort of general ordering principle, particularly in the social sphere religion tends to be transformed in the mentality of Christians into a scaled-down collection of gestures and rites where the presence of God is only perceived in the most ephemeral manner possible. Or, in another example, religion is transformed into the theosophical religion, the seat of a God reduced to a mythical, inconsistent entity ready to take all forms.

We find concrete existence replaced everywhere by abstraction, disjunction, the disembodied idea, having no connection with what is real, natural or supernatural, human or divine. "I see modern man pass by, with an idea of himself and the world, no longer a set idea," aptly writes Valéry, [13] that is, translated into our own vocabulary, who is no longer the incarnation of an idea.

---

12 A time of upheaval as the French connotes.
13 *Cahiers*, 1894.

ABSTRACTION AND INSTINCT

This first phenomenon is automatically accompanied by a second. What is abstract and disconnected, and an ideology-based awareness of reality, are incapable of motivating man. They are only a conduit, a framework, an outlet, to be filled with the uncertain forces, brutal and unhealthy, of instinct left to itself. What is man actually left with in order to navigate life, except the tentacles of instinct and the antennas of feelings? Every disembodiment is fatally accompanied by a concomitant animalization. If reason is unconstrained, the brute is equally unconstrained. The law in our age is thus abolished by an oscillating movement which, with equal impetus, hurls man from one extreme to the other, from the rational to the irrational and back. Here we might enlarge on this by looking at some examples of this contamination of instinct by ideology, and of ideology by instinct: liberalism and an egotistical instinct; egalitarianism and the impulse to imitate; state socialism and the gregarious instinct; Freudianism and the sexual instinct; pacifism and the instinct of self-defense, which is fear; the moral code of the superman and the instinct to dominate, to take aggressive measures; Marxism and the appetite for food . . . We could thus explain the incredible combination of abstract love for the people, humanity, the proletariat, and the use of cruelty towards them, but we must limit ourselves to these remarks.

SCIENCE AND CIVILIZATION

We have set aside until now the matter of science and its influence on people today, because it is the absolutely typical example. We will not dwell here on the fetishism and idolatry of science, characteristic of our time. It is undeniable that science and the mythical representation most men make of it have profoundly disrupted societal customs.

Let us recall the famous words of Bergson, "the body of man aggrandized by science has need of a supplement from the soul."[14] Projected onto the field of our contemporary way of life, this expression is extraordinarily enlightening, if it is explained in a sense doubtlessly not Bergsonian. For we can ask whether the human body with the prodigious stature given to it through science and technology, which prolong its life, is capable of receiving a supplement from the soul. On the contrary, to make matters worse, everything transpires as if the soul remained outside of man, immobilized by formulaic reasoning whose role is to encompass and direct, like a machine, the world and all sectors of existence on earth. No longer elevated inwardly by a soul incarnate in it, the human body, aggrandized by science, and the world in which the body participates are turned into dust, into an aggregate of watertight grains of sand, into an intricate machinery which a devitalized, mechanized reason now manages from outside this process. One could say, returning to the expression of Bergson, that the spirit of the man aggrandized by science needs a supplement of vitality. But the conclusion is the same: science, as it is assimilated by the psychology of contemporary man, bears down on humanity in order to reduce it to its schemas.

Here is a first series of resulting facts: the more human reason strives to despoil the world of its secrets through meticulous, exact techniques, the more man himself, this concrete being of flesh and blood, thrust into the world through his body and incarnate nature, is uprooted and eludes his condition of a living being. Thus everything happens as though the transformation of the world into "scientific concepts" and rational blueprints, which eliminate all opacity and thanks to which man can act in the world in unequaled security, were validated, due to the exhaustion of human vitality and an ever more distressing inability to grasp the concrete values of friendship, closeness to others, and a spirit of cordial cooperation, values

---

14 De Corte here paraphrases words of Bergson with this meaning, from *Les Deux Sources de la morale et de la science*, 1932.

that are supported in the world provided that man is open to their influence. As a consequence, man no longer seems to live as part of the world, with the creatures in it and with his brothers and sisters, except by closing himself to openness to others. Placed in the world, side by side with others, our contemporaries are no longer organically bound together. They are in constant need of exterior forces to join together, like the cogwheels of a machine, in order to function. This explains the attraction exercised over them by all forms of state control and totalitarianism.

Here is another in the series of consequences: in the measure to which modern science coordinates all its efforts and its investment in the world, with the goal of extracting all its mysteries and reducing them to intelligible formulas, it simultaneously tends to replace the concrete entities which are its subject with a series of abstract, universal facts which constitute the object of its research. This is how our vision of man and the material world has become increasingly lifeless, disembodied, cast into ever more rigid forms, of which contemporary society gives us many sinister examples. We are placed in a world where life seems to have withdrawn, and where its concrete elements have little by little been taken up and swept away in a relentless movement, into the wheels of a machine whose ideologies are joined to systems, theories to plans, numerical data to files, statistics to censuses, doctrinaire concepts to utopias, bureaucratic decrees to administrative procedures, ending with the decisive transformation of man into a robot, which our descendants, if they are wise, will consider the most comical catastrophe in the history of humanity. We are witnessing a metamorphosis of what is human, which we should not hesitate to label a falsification.

MORAL CONSEQUENCES

Morality in man has been completely reversed. Instead of being directed, with the unconscious spontaneity of traditional customs, towards a concrete end considered good or bad, it is thrust into a kind of wild flight away from what is real, towards abstractions, products of an overexcited human mind, and confronted with genuine idols, capitalized: Sex, Race, Work, the People, the Nation, Socialism, Democracy, Capital, the Law, Liberty, Civilization (I list these in random order), sometimes even endowed with a dazzling pharisaism concealing an astonishing underlying hypocrisy, affecting the human person. Such are the abstract, rational, and logical goals, the pure ideas which modern man pursues and which he tries to make his own by means of a coherent use of reason, calculation, enumeration, estimation, computation, establishment of rules, and knowledge and assessment of basic causes and effects, and of the responses of instincts to stimuli. Certain promoters of this new morality (I am speaking of politicians because the *homo politicus* is an enlarged image of modern man), where the passion for ideas replaces the patient action of shared moral standards and the respect for exemplary behavior, have become experts in the use of apt methods for diverting human beings from the concrete ends assigned to them by nature and for propelling them towards the pursuit of fabrications of the mind and abstract concepts concealing a swarm of the most disordered appetites: envy, hatred, concupiscence, deception, lying, the will to obtain power, egoism, *Schadenfreude*, [15] and a perverse taste for vacuousness, carefully camouflaged as logical, ideological principles of conduct. These are reasoned out in clubs, lodges, gatherings of every kind, even in special schools opened in certain countries at government expense.

As for the results of this undertaking, they are laid out before our eyes in their tragic breadth, multiplied by a thousand and one rationally managed strategies for propaganda, at the disposal of the new man and new morality in order

---

15   Pleasure derived from another's misfortune.

to reach their perfection. In the modern world, the least human contact with one's fellow man and the least pursuit of a concrete human goal, such as the love of neighbor, family, work, fatherland, and God Himself, tend to become impossible. These are in short order replaced by what is called the organization, sprung not from life, experience, history, or an intensifying force with roots in the past, but from the mind and the intoxicating power which it releases.

DISSOCIATIVE RATIONALISM

The vast movement which drags man towards an exhaustive rationalization of his being and behavior can only be explained by an alteration of what is essential in him, taking place in the course of these last centuries and which we propose calling, for want of a better word, rationalism. It is not a matter of commonplace rationalism, the definition of which, it has been agreed, refers to a movement of liberation of the mind with regard to religious dogmas. Still less does it concern philosophical rationalism, but a rationalism, sharp and cutting as a blade, which has penetrated to the invisible center of man's being, the origin of his everyday behavior, and has disassociated the components of his nature and the principles of his actions.

Man is a singular animal. There are within him immense, permanent possibilities for estrangement, unknown in other species. Placed at the top of the biological hierarchy, his instability is the price to be paid for his excellence. While other living beings follow their straightforward path and the trajectory of their existence, with no other loss except death, man bears within himself, in his own existence, the innate capacity for dissolution. If we use the term "mind"[16] to denote the ensemble of rational faculties by means of which man stands outside the world, dominates it and understands it, and the term "life" to denote the mysterious complex of sense-based and emotional roots

---

16   *Esprit* in French, denoting mind, as well as spirit or soul.

which he plunges into the world in order to benefit from what they bring him, it must be said that these complementary elements of human nature which draw on each other, interpenetrating each other and working simultaneously, are only too rarely united. Here the normal is exceptional. It is not excessive to claim that the history of humanity, viewed as a whole, obeys a kind of cyclical law of alternating equilibrium and rupture between the mind and life. Man becomes integrated into an authentically human existence when mind and life are brought together in him. He dies when these are separated. But the birth and agony of man and civilizations are terribly long and their periods of maturity excessively brief. One thinks of the amusing and bitter popular proverb: "Teeth, but no nuts; nuts, but no teeth." So it is too often in human history where the mind and human vitality are hardly ever proportionate to each other in spite of their respective appeals to man: Too much intellect, not enough vitality; too much vitality, not enough intellect. What we have elsewhere called the incarnation of man is without doubt an arc which only joins itself to form a perfect circle in a posthumous, indescribable state, what the Church defines obscurely in her doctrine on the resurrection of the body.

Where do we find ourselves now? Are we in the ascending or descending stage in the spiral of human life? Do we still have enough vitality to join body and soul to the world and to commune with it in order to aspire to a rosy future along with the worshipers of progress? How could man, under the influence of no matter what system or ideology, reconstruct all of his tottering civilization since he himself is not whole. If the world is "broken", isn't this because man himself is broken first? We are at the same time the prey of the most scientific utopias and the most amorphous instincts. Our whole being feels the attraction of the most untenable abstract projects and the blind impulses of our animal nature.

Man today is made up of a strange combination of Don Quixote and Sancho Panza, but each denuded of the charm given them by Cervantes, and terribly degraded. We are torn apart, on the cross formed by our devitalized spirit and our despiritualized life, a condition incapable of being in harmony with the noble laws, simple, consecrated by history, which rule the existence of man in the world. The spirit of modern man tends to function independently of his vitality, which complements the spirit and is alone capable of situating it in a relationship with the concrete world, itself endowed with a spirit and innate intelligibility. This division, so typical today, explains how the mind, denuded of its vital complement, is filled with abstractions of every kind which, stripped of every concrete human meaning, are interlocked in a formal ideological determinism which integrates them, as antagonistic as they may be to one another, into the same inhuman common denominator. This also explains how life, deprived of the presence of the spirit enduring in it, becomes dull, sclerotic, limited to the material, and then only capable of communicating with the world in a mechanized, blind manner.

AN IDEOLOGICAL CANCER

No aspect of the world has been unaffected by this phenomenon of the disembodiment of the spirit and the animalization of life. A reversal in the structure of man is occurring: the mind, not grafted onto life and the concrete, becomes swollen and distended like an edema caused by a nutritional deficiency, while the possibility of any intuition about the world and the interrelatedness of man and the world diminishes to the point of disappearing. It matters little whether the "ideas" which then prey on man are ill-formed or ingenious, cynical or naive, stupid or rational, vague or mathematically determined, what is essential is their common state of disconnectedness, their working as a closed circuit, always hostile towards *what is*, their fundamental inability to commune with objective reality and to emerge from human experience; we have here the rupture of any bonds springing from life which might connect ideas to the man of flesh and blood and to the world.

We cannot resist the comparison with cancer here. We know that cancerous cells are themselves anarchical and free, so to speak, from the law of complementarity and from the mutual interaction among cells which rules the organism. They proliferate apart from the rest of the body, while draining it of energy and exhausting its substance. Armed with an unusual power to multiply, though they are foreign to the organism which harbors them, they take it over and kill it. So it is with the "ideas" which have broken with the laws inherent in the world and in man. In every period of decline, they literally live off humanity like parasites, under one form or another: religious, philosophical, artistic, social, political, etc. This image could, moreover, be extended: like biological cancer, ideological cancer has its metastases. As we know well enough today, when a cancerous tumor is removed, traces of it remain which cause it to reappear. Man increasingly tends to relate only to his "ideas" and as he, like them, is separated from the concrete, he lets himself be carried along by them, becomes uprooted from the world, and dies. So have the Greek and Roman types of men disappeared. Likewise threatened with disappearance is the traditional Occidental type of man whom we know and who now only survives in increasingly limited geographical areas.

Examples of this abound. On the level of the individual, look at the bourgeois Christian whose religion is reduced in theory to a form of deism and whose life is a web of passions. Another man, emancipated, cultivates "great principles" and slides down the slopes of all his desires. On the scientific level, there is Freudianism with its reduction of man to the pitiless logic of sex and its defense of the libido, and modern physics with its purely mathematical vision of a world set into equations, and their resulting applications, which fawn upon our death and pleasure instincts. Art escapes into the abstract and only provokes a nervous reaction or sensory overload. Social justice is cast as the heaven of systems of thought, and the egoism of individuals and groups increases. Nations get drunk on myths and activate the most vulgar of man's instincts. Diverted from the task proper to him, which is to instill spirit into life and to humanize the world and himself, contemporary man sees his power of reasoning cut off from all its concrete bonds with both the real and the absolute. He has become an abstraction: *homo sexualis, homo ethnicus, homo oeconomicus, homo civis,* [17] endowed with a destructive logic, subjecting himself and the world to his intransigent apriorism, and abolishing all diversity. Under cover of these abstractions, a multitude of emancipated instincts swarms, escaping from the control of an incarnate spirit which is attentive to life and joined to a new spirit detached from life, and are unleashed onto the world with ever increasing violence. We can predict the inevitable direction of this specifically modern movement: disaster and the abyss, man reduced to a mechanized schema and to his brutal passions, as the new barbarian hordes arise out of a rationalist cauldron.

BEING AND VITALITY

We are in the presence of a mysterious process which operates in every declining civilization and which is found in the disruption of our epoch. Though its scope is difficult to define, it seems to consist of a disaffection between man and himself inasmuch as he is a being in the world, that is to say, as belonging to a world order which he has not established and to which he is united through a thousand invisible ties, rich in exchanges and relationships. This lack of rootedness in the world is precisely the phenomenon of devitalization: man is incapable of being nourished by what is real, and he

---

17 Man as sexual, ethnic, economic, and as a citizen.

compensates for his organic inferiority, his lack of vitality, with a rational system of conduct which places him outside the world, giving him the illusion of dominating it as he gives himself an elevated position. This ends up with both man and the civilization he has constructed being without a place in the world, as both disappear, cast out by the implacable laws of nature, which has been violated.

It is really through life that man succeeds in becoming integrated into the world as it is, without deforming it, through an act of robust adaptation which overcomes all obstacles and maps out a reciprocal harmony between man's power and the laws governing reality. All the specific functions and faculties of man suffer from a certain distance between them and their object, which can only be overcome by their integration into reality. There is in life, however, a power to validate, to adapt, an ability to match information from the senses with objects, of which the direct consequence is the reciprocal relationship between man and the world, the harmony between them, forming an overall unity, which is the indispensable beginning of the metaphysical affirmation of being. This is exactly how vitality surpasses biological categories and the scope of the natural sciences (where a certain rationalist and racist spirit, decadent besides, would aim to fence vitality in) and attains to what must be called, with an inevitably deficient term, the presence of being. [18] It is proper to vitality to accept, not passively or resignedly, but actively and joyously, the conditions of reality right down to their metaphysical roots. Without this nuptial bond between life and the world, without the lived conviction, above all more lived than conceptualized except in certain rare privileged minds, that human destiny is a network of bonds between ourselves and the rest of the

---

18 This term has a commonality with how Heidegger interpreted the German word for existence, *Dasein*, literally "being there". For the German philosopher this meant being-in-the-world, living as engaged with the world and one's fellow human beings.

world, no "idea", unless it be degraded and operating within an artificial, hollow conceptual order, is, strictly speaking, possible. All *vitalized* temperaments which do not flee when faced with reality and which do not construct for themselves a mendacious world which ends up making them comfortable in their weakness, detached from themselves, living within a purely visual image of their impotent aspirations, have felt, penetrating through their dullness and slowness, the immediate presence of the real, which no denial of reality can take away: the degree to which man perceives the world in a straightforward manner is gauged by the degree to which he is open to influences from the world with which life communicates. Let us not delude ourselves into thinking that we have arrived at the limit of an intelligible inquiry on vitality. Nor do we assert that vitality pure and simple, hypothetically isolated from its complement, the intellectual side of man filled with content from his superior faculties, can be raised to this level of inquiry. What is essential in the recovery of the ultimate foundation of our being, which we have briefly attempted here, is that our vital adhesion to the real world, not deformed by our "ideas", is at the same time an affirmation of the sacred nature of our being and of our relegation to an order which we have not constructed and which conditions our human existence because it is part of our makeup. This affirmation of the sacred, far being the result of pure spirituality, is on the contrary placed where what is from above and what is from below coincide, the spiritual and the carnal in man who, experiencing himself as being in the world, experiences at the same time organically forming part of a network of relationships which he has not created and which go beyond him. It is only the devitalized man, separated from the rest of the world by the very reason of his poverty of vitality, who can deny the necessary transcendence of the bonds which the history of humanity – *historia magistra vitae* [19] – brings into existence.

---

19 History is the teacher of life.

The world and the civilization which man develops in it are thus driven not by "ideas" but by man's capacity for vitality and by his religious sentiments regarding his participation in those sole aspects of reality which are incompatible with any attempt to control them completely: respect for life, love of nature, regard for the family, reverence towards the land of one's forebears, a liking for work, acknowledgment of a superior, divine order, in short, the ensemble of concrete relationships which man necessarily experiences – either in a positive manner, accepting them, or in a negative manner, breaking with them – with the persons and things close to him, which form part of his existence and which he himself has created.

TRANSCENDENCE OF THE CONCRETE AND TRANSCENDENCE OF THE ABSTRACT

The feeling of the transcendence of the concrete and of the presence of persons, structures, and organic laws over which we have no control comes *before* any rational knowledge and sustains the entire development of thought. [20] Indeed, we know less about the person who is the locus of our being than we acknowledge, to go back to the expression of Claudel. [21] We acknowledge this with an act of simultaneous recognition and gratitude. [22] Here we have the eternal truth of Platonism. [23] Every civilization which enables man to participate in the reality of the world is founded on lived experience and on the *Erlebnis* [24] of

---

20 Cartesianism, on the contrary, posits the primacy of rational knowledge over being. De Corte's note.
21 Paul Claudel, 1868-1955, eminent French dramatist, poet, essayist, and diplomat. This indirect quote is consonant with the ideas Claudel presents in *L'art poétique*, a treatise expressing his poetical vision of the world, and including a section on knowledge of the world and of one's self.
22 Literally, "an act of *reconnaissance* in its twofold meaning", referring to both connotations of *reconnaissance*, recognition and gratitude.
23 Here De Corte possibly refers to the theme of self-knowledge in Plato, figuring in the *Euthyphro*, the *Ion*, and other dialogues.
24 German philosophical term for experience, with the connotation of an experience not related to concepts, or an ineffable experience.

the organicity of being. This participation is not subject to proof, in the current meaning of the word, where "to prove" essentially means to conceptualize a certain "something" exterior to thought, to reduce the unknown to the known, and to set up a logical, overarching series of facts from which others are deduced and then in turn verified by reason in the same way. The process of testing is indispensable. The whole rational system of a civilization is seen as only having value to the degree that it springs from this fundamental attitude.

The result is that the spiritual and intellectual development of a civilization is not the product of reason, but of the consent of the spirit to the life into which it is incarnated and on which it sheds light on man's capacity for participation in the world, thus increasing his ability for communion with it. If this foundation is lacking, all the rest forms just a weak surface under which swarm the harshest barbarities. Huxley anticipated this in *Brave New World*.[25] From this point of view, a patriarchal civilization which seems down-to-earth, where the sacred nature of being is upheld, even in irrational modes, is superior to the type of civilization we know, where everything contributes to the refusal to give any significance to the sense of the sacred, in the name of a form of thinking which is becoming increasingly disembodied. We know this from common sense, which judges the humble Chinese peasant, warm and open, perhaps through superstition, to be at a higher level than the learned Western economic strategist, closed to any tendency to be merciful, a tendency until recently considered one of the essential attributes of civilized life by unanimous popular agreement. In spite of his outrageous diatribes, Rousseau is a better judge here than Voltaire: if he is mistaken about the meaning of "nature", which he continually evokes and

---

25 Dystopian novel satirizing the exaltation of science, with its dehumanizing effects. Aldous Huxley, 1894-1963, British, prolific author of novels, essays, and poetry.

defines according to the anarchical tendency of his drives, he has rightly denounced the artifices of a century less rationalist than ours as the worst way to dissolve societies and true civilization. The Encyclopedists were not wrong in going after him in their hate. [26]

A civilization such as ours, ruled through the unconditional primacy of the intellect, was bound to completely overturn social relations, substituting the principle of egalitarianism for the principle of organic diversity. While the work of life proceeds at a varied pace, the spirit separated from life operates according to an unchangeable tempo. The trees of the forest do not all grow in the same way, some are small, others are tall; rivers have their twists and turns; no animal looks exactly like another of the same species . . . But all telephone poles are the same, standing upright; canals also are as straight as possible; drinking glasses identical to each other are mass produced . . . Where the disembodied spirit insinuates itself, it introduces a conceptual norm, which effaces all differences: all men are equal because the same concept applies to them all; one man is equal to another; "good sense is the best distributed thing in the world . . . . " [27] With this as an objective, the universality of good sense would obviously have the power to disorganize a society, since the organization of a society implies differentiation, hierarchy, and subsidiarity. This is why in a paradox, which only seems to be one, the devitalized intellect universalizes and individualizes at the same time: to claim to be the equal of others, one must become totally separated from them, without retaining any common bond. Egalitarianism and individualism are the twin faces of a single process of disassociation which stabilizes the scattered members of the social body by means of one

---

26 Participants in an Eighteenth-century revolutionary movement beginning in France. The Encyclopedists heralded endless progress through science and called for freedom from religious beliefs, considered superstitious.
27 Descartes, *Discours de la méthode*, 1637.

concept, nation, race, work, consumption, humanity, as it happens it matters little which one. The essential thing here is the uprooting common to these various ways of casting man outside his organic context and, in parallel manner, the birth of an abstraction in the depths of his intellect – no matter which one, since they are all nonexistent – which intellectualizes and universalizes this rupture. The distinctive characteristic of man cut off from his roots is actually to cease existing organically and to form a self-image based on an idea about himself: the rootless man proves himself incapable of experiencing the presence of the real, from which he is separated; he *imagines* himself in the only way left to him, within a setting, that is, an abstract concept. It matters little, once again, whether this concept is subtle or coarse, scientific or common, concise or elaborated imaginatively. The most important thing here is the minimalist, simplistic character of the concept. Not having arisen from a life directly in touch with what is real, concepts in all their manifestations are imbued with unreality, which has a powerful, magnetic attraction. Whatever its capacity, the intellect here works against real existence, so the mind, having no rootedness, amputated from life, is at the same time hampered in the act of thinking where it reveals itself: it can neither perceive reality nor interpret it. Completely detached from his roots, man can only act under the combined pressure of his instincts and superficial slogans, which create a kind of debased spirit in him as universal and widespread as it is empty of content, bordering on nothingness. We recognize all these persons, bursting with automatic reflex reactions and formulaic expressions, whose numbers are increasing throughout the world as they wreak devastation. The planet is full of them.

Now a self-image which is no longer connected to life and the reality with which we coexist is an absolute, strictly independent of everything which is not itself: it is a transcendence of the abstract, diametrically opposed to the transcendence of the concrete, of structures which preexist thought. Man builds his empire on this abstract idea of transcendence because it is in line with his diminished existence. From such a perspective, man transcends himself: the image he has of himself dominates him and determines all his initiatives. However, this process is only possible to the degree that the abstract image of man can be manipulated like a tool which transforms matter, that is to say inasmuch as each individual coming to the scene of history identifies with it so that it directs his acts: it is after all clear that an abstraction cannot act. To affirm the transcendence of man with respect to himself is thus also to affirm that man is in his essence a being who makes conquests. It is not a matter here of an interior conquest nor of self-mastery, since the individual is from the outset engulfed by his self-image: on the contrary it is a matter of gaining control over others. The man cut off from his roots is dedicated to transforming others according to his own ideas. This necessarily becomes widespread; it can only be contagious. The more he *puts forward an image of himself*, the more he must impose this image on others, discovering his image in all of humanity, as in a multi-sided mirror which infinitely multiplies his self-representation. To attain this goal, universal individualism – let us take note of this conjunction of opposites – finds powerful allies in science, which impersonalizes, and in technology, which standardizes. It might even perhaps be necessary to ask oneself if the rising tide of science and technology which is submerging current civilization does not have its origin in the very structure of contemporary man, instead of being itself, as commonly believed, the cause of his transformation. This is why we see the ideologies of today invoking the prestige of science and technology, while denying, secretly or brazenly, any significance to metaphysics, which places man at the heart of his destiny and confronts him personally with the concrete transcendence of the Creator. Among the various branches of science, none are more audacious than biology, economics, and political science, which, moreover, work in partnership. The reason for this is clear: they have a bearing on relationships which people form among themselves, and thus prove more apt than any of the other sciences to destroy the fundamental structures against which humanity has never dared, according to the expression of Plato, to raise a hand to commit parricide. [28] Contemporary man is literally saturated with all this: it is enough to look at the place accorded to these sciences in the newspapers all over the world, as well as in the education of children; it particularly suffices to look at their profound influence on the concerns of those in charge of governments. We could say that the problems of health, production, consumption, and public opinion constitute a sort of way to penetrate the "soul" of man today in order to influence it with consummate ease. Those who control the masses are compelled to supply them with information which rescues them from the bonding of two opposite poles, the individual and the world. The transcendence of man over himself comes at this cost: if each individual is in good health, if his levels of production and consumption are normal, if he expresses his opinion of where the body politic is headed, what else could he desire? His "life" is assured along with the "lives" of all the others: a top-notch, well-regulated hygienic approach in each of these areas will work wonders . . . The transcendence of man does not reach a very high level . . .

CIVILIZATION OF THE MASSES

A pseudo-civilization ruled by a system of disembodied ideas, themselves underpinned and fed by instincts even more devitalized and mechanized, reveals what Ortega y

---

28 Apparently a reference to the *Sophist*, where a character, the stranger from Elea, questions the ideas of Parmenides, some of which Plato, a kind of intellectual father, shared, and asks his interlocutor not to take the inquiry as a "parricide." Thus the questioning of ideological structures would be a metaphorical form of parricide.

Gasset has justly termed the *masses*.[29] The mass-man is situated at the point where the current rationalist civilization is coming to an end. He is essentially a spirit who has broken the bonds connecting him to experiential reality beneath him and to non-perceptible reality above him. He is an unwieldy abstraction who, as he falls, is degraded and astonishingly resembles the atom of Epicurean physics, with his own *clinamen*[30] – in this case the vision of an earthly paradise offered to him by his leaders –which attaches him to other atoms, causing them to be aggregated. Nothing on the surface of earth holds him back in his descent; he is like a rock which falls and knocks against the hard, impenetrable soil. The mass-man is destined to land in a world which he considers malleable, as though devoid of any kind of solidity, which he molds with the help of debased techniques which procure a *civilization* for him where he can construct a "new world" in tune with all his stratagems. Born in a rationalist civilization, today he leads it through all its metamorphoses: to become convinced of this, one only has to look at the absurd, ruinous goals to which he directs the huge enterprises resulting from the inventions of contemporary science and technology. What has become, in the hands of the mass-man, of radio and other means of communication, cinema, and nuclear fission, to limit ourselves to major inventions? The only response to be given, unreservedly, is that these are

29 José Ortega y Gasset, 1883-1955, Spanish philosopher and essayist whose best-known work, *La rebelión de las masas* (1930), criticized the mediocrity of the masses and what he termed the "tyranny of the majority". He used the term "mass-man", taken up by De Corte, as representative of the masses.
30 *Clinamen*, Latin for "inclination". A term used by Lucretius (c. 99-c. 55 BC), Roman poet and philosopher, to defend the theories of the Greek philosopher Epicurus (341-270 BC). It refers to the raining down of atoms into the void at the beginning of the world. When the trajectory of some of these atoms becomes oblique (inclined), in the powerful force of their descent they knock against each other and join together, thus forming beings. De Corte refers to the vision of an earthly paradise as a kind of *clinamen*, a force which causes people to bind together in groups in the decline of civilization.

instruments of the destruction of the spiritual life. It is the same with the parallel effort which aims to liberate the individual, peoples, races, all humanity and which finds expression in so-called democratic institutions, which go in the direction of servitude everywhere. Through a slow evolution or the outbreak of a revolution, the mass-man, breaking his organic bonds which life has formed in the course of centuries and which provide open lines of communication between the mind and emotions and the world, constructs another world where, under the cover of words increasingly devoid of meaning, he puts in place the most frightening nihilism history has ever known. Let us stress here the major changes which technology and science have undergone since the eighteenth century: oriented in the beginning towards creating harmony between man and the world, they are becoming, in the hands of the mass-man and his leaders, instruments of a general depersonalization which uproots the human being and the world from the concrete and causes his descent into a future more and more deprived of its axes, where men and things ceaselessly succeed each other, with a total lack of individual character: style in modern life is precisely the absence of style. Similarly, one observes the close relationship between the bursting of the masses onto the scene of history and the weakening of the family, trades and professions, regions and countries, churches, all the organic social bodies which give man his character, customs, instinctive reactions, differentiation from others, and a particular personality. In this abstract, ravaged humanity we find the mass-man, whose character is not to have one, since the same character is found in each person, simply consisting of a concept not adulterated by the presence of the real, an idea repeated in an infinite number of examples and enjoying a specious ubiquity, having nothing proper to itself because it is devoid of content, as it lets man descend with all his weight into the animal nature of the herd. It is a fluid, inconsistent, and amorphous idea, continually in the process of coming into being, as it becomes disembodied. In such an atmosphere the human personality, fruit of man's incarnation in the world and constitutive of his character, becomes a pure grammatical fiction: the "I", "you", and "we" disappear to the benefit of the universal "they".

As Max Picard has well discerned,[31] the mass-man is also the man who flees from reality and, in the end, from God, Lord of the real. Engrossed in his ideologies and in the artificial world they construct, where he never meets with any obstacle, the mass-man is engaged in an endless flight which takes his ability to transform reality to the limit. Cut off from his living roots, he develops to the maximum his ability to subject the world to a project of devitalization and oversimplification, with his empty formulaic verbiage, where words become like a dead leaves blown about by the wind. The world in which man flees from reality is linear, geometric, and quantifiable, beyond words, where every nuance is abolished within a uniform structure. Thus the mass-man is obliged to transform the real, always characterized by diversity, into a homogeneous, unchangeable image, and to eliminate the last traces of the natural institutions of the former variegated civilization: family, trades and professions, towns and villages, regions, etc., which are in opposition to his boundless desire to erase distinctions. This is the beginning of the transformation of reality into an artificial construct which we call "the wonders of technology". This transformation can never come to a stop precisely because it is a flight from the real, and only the real can serve as a destination. Here we have one of the major causes of the modern mystique of unlimited progress, endlessly in motion, engaging in dialectics in a world where everyone turns his back on any commitment and refuses to acknowledge that anything

---

31   1888-1965, Swiss writer and philosopher, author of *The Flight from God*, 1934.

could be permanent. Yet this flight actually serves as the most appropriate centrifugal force[32] which could allow the mass-man to build a new civilization for himself: because the flight is in a straight line, with no deviations, it carries everything along with it with incredible ease; because it has no end point, it can claim to satisfy all human desires, even contradictory ones. As strange as this paradox may appear, the disembodied civilization characteristic of the mass-man thus becomes a civilization where everything becomes material destined to be continually transformed as it flees from what is real. It is by considering reality under its most physical aspect and by converting it into something only material that it becomes entirely possible to flee from it and to transform it into a new world with a constant propensity to take flight. When what is real is identified with matter, it requires a new form which from now on only man is capable of giving it and which will constantly evolve according to the trajectory of his flight. There is no longer anything which still remains of the original bond between man and authentic existence, no connections which impede his flight, nothing that is determined independently of man. The disembodied idea that man makes of himself, which is identified with his flight from reality, can from now on impose itself on a world become wholly material, in order to transform it into a new world.

In this world where man flees from reality, *in a descent*, we witness a singular phenomenon, the identification of opposites. While an organic civilization of normal people brings together a variety of individuals and groups sharing a living unity of spirit and a common destiny, the inorganic civilization of the mass-man brings about, in its flight from reality, the coexistence of the most opposite concepts. This confusion is hardly astonishing since the flight from

---

32   In the sense of propelling man away from the center, from reality.

reality effectuates the identification of the one with the many, and of the individual with panic.[33]

First of all, the civilization of the mass-man assimilates the incorporeal into the material. In no earlier civilization, even in one with the games of the circus, do we notice such a mixture of abstract ideology and insatiable desires, of escape towards faceless entities: Justice, Peace, Work, Liberty, etc., and of getting bogged down in the desire for material goods, moreover of a lower and lower quality. On the one hand, the mass-man conceives of himself as unidimensional as possible: *homo civis, homo oeconomicus, homo ethnicus, homo rationalis*, etc., who sets himself up as an example of the flight from everyday life where soul and body work, struggle, love, and think in a complex world, in touch with relatives, one's spouse, children, neighbors, friends, familiar landscapes, the various reflections of the Creator spread over the whole world. On the other hand, the mass-man is strongly attracted to sensational newspaper headlines, vile pictures in magazines, the cinema, political demonstrations, big sporting events, "entertainment", and news on the radio, in short, he rushes headlong into a wasted world, from the first glance obviously debased, where he kills time after hours spent at his boring, mechanized job. The essence of matter, understood properly, is in effect to be flat, with no depth, and to be limited to merely tactile perception. It is curious in this regard to observe how the visual stimuli of the cinema and the audio of the radio are really shocks to the senses, creating sensory overload. It is the same with all the sensory stimulation in the big cities where the mass-man congregates. In fact, the material world, deprived of soul and life, is a world characterized by flatness, beneath which there is *nothing*. It is a world where people no longer have living roots and in which they have become incapable

---

33   Possibly De Corte means here that the existence of an individual not identified with the mass-man elicits a reaction of panic, as an unpredictable phenomenon.

of penetrating to the depths of the nourishing substance of the real. There is no longer the least physical complexity in it. Its elements glance off the surface of the skin when the sense of touch comes into play. For matter is in itself impenetrable by *default*: it is the bottom-most layer which covers over the void. In this sense, it imitates a sheet of metal fashioned by a power hammer: matter receives the basic form projected onto it by a disembodied ideology which, joined to it, produces a series of artificial settings where a type of man evolves who is condemned to live on the surface of himself, at the level of his materiality. This is, again, the world where man flees from reality, where there is only a crude tactile sense, a groping about to find one's way. What is most profound in modern man, as Valéry said with bitterness, is his skin . . . . [34]

Secondly, the civilization of the mass-man is inextricably entwined with the most intransigent dogmatism and the most changeable interpretations of events. Since there is no criterion with which to assess reality, civilization flees at one and the same time in the direction of intransigence and variability. It resembles a weather vane, which, though stationary, rotates as the wind blows. This is what certain philosophers modestly call "dialectic". In reality, this dialectic in which man engages, successively uniting opposites in an unchallenged method, is the endpoint of rationalism and the point of the rupture between spirit and life which characterizes this civilization. To build a new world which lets him function as he continues along his path, a world which can only be born from his cogitation, debased to the level of slogans and words emitted like burps, the mass-man is doomed to change his apriorism endlessly, *without doing away with it*. With no basis for assessing his efforts and drawing from them a standard for future action, he tells himself that he is the measure of everything—that is part of what he calls his humanism—elevating himself above

---

34   *L'idée fixe*, 1931.

the world that he fashions, but at the same time and in
the same way, evolving in a trajectory of pure, ever fluc-
tuating possibility. His rationalism is fluid, his implacable
logic evolves nonstop, in an utterly formalistic way, in the
course of daily happenings and events. Neither "yes" nor
"no" has any more meaning for him except with regard to
his will to dominate the world he is building. This is why
the mass-man jumps from one theory to another with ease,
provided that these are entirely ideological. In the same
way, his nature, characterized by formalism, accommodates
itself to what is openly Machiavellian, where reversals in
opinion are beyond reckoning. Every approach becomes a
pretext for domination, and this back-and-forth from one
extreme to another, as much on the ideological level as on
the practical, contributes to the breakup of the last remains
of reality, which the mass-man must destroy in order to
exercise his domination. This is why he venerates without
distinction legalism, governmental power, administrative
paperwork, and the bureaucratic and military state: these
empty, imperious forms which are modeled on a world
in a state of agitation constitute for him modes of escape,
thanks to which he compensates for his uprootedness and
develops his inborn ambition to have absolute power over
everything. At the first stage of this hollow formalism of
the mass-man, one always finds his emptiness and the
endless delusions which he imposes on a soulless world,
while believing in a perfect future resembling the trajectory
of his flight: nothing is beyond me, nothing is impossible.
The more Utopian a project is, the more it fascinates him.

Finally, the civilization of the mass-man combines space
and time into one category, the future. Marx characterized
this attribute in his astonishing statement, *The future of
man is man*,[35] supreme expression of man's flight from
reality. Mass-man casts himself outside himself, and away

---

35 For an atheist who saw man primarily from the point of view of
economics, called to engage in class struggle, this position is inevitable.

from the specific space and time which enclose his present existence into a future extending over the whole planet: his governing principle, universal and abstract in character, obliges him to do this. He is incapable of enduring his present life in the here and now. Thus he takes refuge in a constant deployment of demands, discontent, and myths, in his dream of an earthly paradise where he would obtain his due. In the same way, he emigrates to the bosom of vast conglomerations of people, where overcrowding with little privacy tends to obliterate space, where people occupy interchangeable positions, where an abundance of distractions uproots them from a life truly lived and an objective sense of time, where time, divided into blocks in the daily routine, becomes just a tool of everyday life. Mass-man is incapable of being himself in the *hic et nunc*[36] of existence. Because he is without roots, he is everywhere, without family, fatherland, or any concrete attachments, absorbed into "humanity". His susceptibility to contagion comes precisely from his denial of space. On the other hand, since he says "no" to everything that came before him, to everything that is "outdated, behind the times, retrograde," rejecting age-old wisdom like last year's car model – and everything that does not answer to his dissatisfaction – he is left with only the future dimension. This typical attitude (for example, the psychology of the mass-man, influenced by the forecasts of scientists and technicians) can be explained by the fact that only the future can be *mathematically calculated*. For the mass-man, not having roots, had no goal: thus he has to submit his existence to the method most denuded of purpose, computation. The mass-man, uncouth or refined, always prepares the way mathematically for "his project": he determines necessary quantities, measures them out, and assesses how the project will develop over time and how it will affect his self-image in the future. Even its savaging effects are known ahead of time: if he does not

---

36 Latin, here and now.

calculate them, others do it for him. The future, which has no actual existence and no specific substance, is in the position of being mechanized ahead of time, all ready to be shaped by the human project, with the assessment of all the data at the disposal of the mass-man admitting of no error. The process of devitalization is here taken to the maximum and then replaced by a series of cogwheels set in automatic motion. This is what some call "the flow of history". Under this carapace the mass-man gives shelter to his destitution, his fundamental incapacity to be himself and to make provision for his life, which he calls an apotheosis.

This is the profound meaning of this civilization: an attempt to make the absolute *refer only to this world*, due to the inability of people to live out a relationship with absolute, on which they are dependent. This failed relationship has the essential property not only of suppressing the impulse which forges a bond with the absolute, but above all of making itself supreme, part of a temporal device capable of obtaining *earthly perfection*. In other words, we have an "upside-down world", or a "permanent revolution". The relationship of man with the absolute is replaced by the withdrawal of man into himself, as his life becomes totally mechanized, just as an act of breathing requires an iron lung when the individual can no longer take in air. Thus perfection is automatically achieved without the least human effort. Whence we have the definition of the mass-man: man is the absolute mechanization of all his human acts.

As we have said elsewhere,[37] "at the same time that he distinguishes between spirit and life, consequently losing the sense of any transcendence, the mass-man at the same time creates to his advantage a new form of the state which has developed to titanic proportions, as we witness. The modern state, whose power has immediate, violent repercussions, from one part of society to another, is a creation of the mass-man, adapted to his mechanical, rationalist,

---

37   Source not given.

soulless mentality, and which he imagines really belongs to him. In the face of the difficulties of life, great and small, the mass-man has recourse to the state and the colossal means at its disposal, with which the mass-man has provided it, in his inertia. So that everything can function automatically, in step with his mechanized life, the mass-man tolerates all necessary sacrifices: with the greatest of ease he allows constraints on his activities, despotism, slavery. He aims for his own apotheosis in the state, and in order to become divine, to affirm his own transcendence, he goes as far as eliminating in himself any remaining humanity. The state thus conceived gives to the mass-man, as to a god, the promise of a life free from anxiety, in which he can have everything: this is the happiness of the mass-man, especially when it is accompanied by the conviction that he is the 'master', that his leaders are his premier servants, a conviction endlessly bruited about by the parasites which every decadent society bears within it. In return, the mass-man makes much of the state, takes care of it, then considers it as a god, the giver of all good things, and if these things are evil, then as the giver of all the evil which nevertheless must be endured in order to attain to the greatest possible happiness possible. Here we see, in all its perfection, the phenomenon of a twofold parasitism where the mass-man is sustained by the state and the state is upheld by the mass-man. Such is the modern conception of civilization, as symbolized by the Catoblepas."[38]

PERSPECTIVES

And now what should we do? We believe profoundly with Proudhon[39] that rationalist civilization is destined

---

38 Mythical animal of Greek and Roman legend, large and bull-shaped, whose head was always turned downward due to its great weight. Its stare or breath could be lethal.
39 Pierre-Joseph Proudhon, 1809–1865, French socialist philosopher and economist, considered to be the father of anarchism, though later in life he advocated for a decentralized government. He criticized many aspects of a statist society.

to disappear. Its increasing rigidity during the last several decades is the prelude to its death. We will not venture to probe into the future or the catastrophes which could be brewing. We are not pessimists in this regard. We gladly echo the words of Bernanos, "It is not because of my despair that I reject the modern world. I reject it because of my great hope."[40] We know that one form of civilization succeeds another and that life always wins out. Regarding the form of civilization which we can and must be working on, even if we belong to the lost generations, "our foresight does not go beyond the antithesis suggested by the present," as Proudhon wrote.[41] It is not a matter of being anti-modern or of preaching a return to the past: one does not ask a sick person to go back to the age he was when he was healthy, but to recover from his illness and get his strength back! It is not a matter, then, of being anti-modern but of saving the modern world, of instilling in it healthy customs, supportive of life, and of eliminating all the works of death from within it. This will not be easy. In fact, we have reached the point where the sclerosis of vitality, the loss of a sense of living in communion with the world, and the rejection of a sense of reverence towards people and things are no longer merely negative phenomena which wear away at the human and leave intact some reserves of vitality capable of bursting forth with an upsurge of energy at a later stage.

Old civilizations died because of the disjunction between the mind and life, although the reserves of life-giving energy were still considerable and made possible the advent of another civilization developing from the earlier one. At the heart of these civilizations, the religious bond linking man to the world and to his origin had not been completely

---

40 Georges Bernanos, 1888-1948, French novelist, essayist, and polemicist best known for his novel *The Diary of a Country Priest*, 1936. The citation may be found in "Articles et témoinages publiés par Bernanos entre 1932 et 1948" in *Scandale de la Vérité*, collected by Romain Deblue, 2019.
41 *Correspondance de P-J Proudhon*, vol. 4, 1875.

destroyed, since due to a lack of adequate technical means the civilizations had not succeeded in taking hold of man completely and remaking him. What is more, beyond their geographic sphere of influence, there were immense stores of energy. It is not the same today. Civilization, having reached its technical apogee and dying of internal wasting away, has shown itself apt, by virtue of its expansion over the whole world and its means of universal penetration, to go from the negative to the positive through a sort of dialectical leap into the realm of the absolute.[42] A tactic of unequaled perfection claims for itself all the contours of a vanished human vitality. This tactic automatically fills in the gaps caused by all the substitutes which progressively denature man, and replaces *homo sapiens* with another type of man, *homo rationalis*, never before seen in history, with no bonds to what is living or to religion. This broken-down vitality gives way to an intensification of a technically oriented mentality which overloads instincts for which the presence of the sacred is nothing but a void, instincts whose outlets are pleasure and domination. Such a situation is grave, but it is not a dead end. We know as certain that the great anonymous collectivities created by social rationalism are destined to devour each other and disappear. History bears witness to this. Where they still remain, they only survive by virtue of the vital energy belonging to the concrete communities, not yet annihilated, which sustain them.

Against opposing winds and rising tides, we must aim for the reestablishment and adaptation to current conditions of these reality-based communities, where by continual communication among themselves people feel a mutual responsibility for each other and are linked by their common destiny. Relatively small social cells like the family,

---

42   Probably a reference to Hegel, who, in his *Encyclopedia of Philosophical Sciences* (1817, revised 1827 and 1830) explains how his dialectical process, a continual synthesizing of opposites, tends toward the "Absolute," the final, all-encompassing concept in whatever branch of knowledge, logic, ethics, politics, etc.

small businesses, labor unions, communities, and regions, where people are in mutual relationship and available to each other, serve as a preparation for a flowering of future social relations, on a larger scale, which will be all the more cohesive if these earlier bonds are safeguarded. A living society follows the law of reciprocal interdependence which holds for every life: in a living body, as it grows, the most diverse organs always operate together, mutually supporting each other. However, let us not succumb to a grave error which consists of considering the problem of civilization from an exclusively moral point of view, which would end by dividing the world into disparate blocks: conservatives with their sense of order, progressives with their justice, Christians with their charity. . . We do not deny the importance of the moral aspect of a society, but consider that it remains, *hic et nunc*, secondary with regard to the devitalization affecting contemporary humanity. What would be the good of a moral order, social justice, or even charity which would provide impoverished persons with the means of camouflaging their destitution? We believe that a certain bourgeois morality and even a certain Christian morality are only masks or bandages covering over a purulent wound. As soon as we propose a "model of man", we look around ourselves and contemplate the ridiculously anemic source from which any possibility of its realization could emerge. How many attempts to regenerate the family, trades and professions, to restore justice or order, to win back the masses to religion, have ended in a stalemate or in the dictatorship of a group of skillful manipulators? Totalitarian systems are proof of this: in order to establish their empire, they prick the conscience of man. "To capture them through idealism" said one of their most famous leaders. [43]

The current crisis is essentially anthropological and, in the last analysis, metaphysical. Let us understand this! The

---

43   A slogan of Lenin's which defined his campaign to propagandize European youth. See *Défense de l'Occident* by Henri Massis, 1927.

metaphysical crisis only affects the human spirit and makes it incapable of relating to transcendent values to the degree that it affects the whole human being in the circumstances of his existence and in his capacity for integration into the real world. Man no longer *sees* transcendent values (without which he cannot exist), quite simply because he no longer *lives* them.

From this point on, just as it is futile to talk about colors to a blind man without the risk of enabling him to think that he cannot make mistakes in that area, it is pointless to set modern man out in pursuit of a spiritual ideal which he will certainly turn into abstractions and lies, if he is incapable of beginning to live it. Then how can we re-create his life, increasingly impoverished? Let us state clearly: it is impossible to re-create a life which has vanished. The man who has broken his bond to what is real will never again be able to reconnect to it, and the devices he employs to survive his inevitable exclusion from what is human are no more than delaying tactics. Life can only be created by life: *omne vivum ex vivo*. [44] Only those who accept life, as weak and deprived as it may be, will be able to transmit and save their civilization. For modern man it is a matter of maintaining, even at the cost of heroism, the hearths where authentic life is found, at the elementary level where it survives today. In this regard, domestic virtues, in spite of their decline, constitute the strongest dynamic reserve we have at our disposal: they conserve the sense of paternal transcendence which could sustain a future framework of other transcendent values which must be recovered. Every life begins from below, from its roots. By and large, man is perhaps only a thinking plant[45] whose roots go deep down to the mysterious springs of life-sustaining nourishment.

---

44 Latin for "all life comes from life."
45 This recalls the words of Pascal, "Man is only a reed, the weakest in nature, but he is a thinking reed." *Penseés, 1670.*

In fact, it is important to consider the original source of life-giving water rather than pursuing a goal. History teaches us that at the birth of civilizations, it is the people full of vitality who undergo the crushing labor of building their subterranean foundations. Only if we are completely realistic, with our feet on the ground, can we gaze on the most distant lodestar. No idealism can take the place of this fundamental requirement. All true idealism, capable of becoming incarnate in man, takes this for granted. This realism has nothing to do with a *Realpolitik* full of false love and methodical violence which we too often see in caricature form. It consists of a realistic view of life and acceptance of its eternal laws, and nothing more. Future generations, if they want to *live*, will turn to the discovery of this realism and this vitality, found in pockets still surviving in the midst of a world ravaged by man, who has misunderstood them.

CHAPTER 2
The Conflict between Politics and Social Issues

OF THE MANY CRACKS WEAKENING the shaky edifice of our civilization, none is more dangerous than the one which disunites the two flying buttresses of collective life, the political and the social.

Popular language, rich in concrete intuitiveness, reveals this to us. We note that these two terms now take on different connotations. The first veers towards the pejorative: "he's a politician", "that's all a matter of politics" . . . In these common phrases one senses a kind of secret repulsion and perhaps even a measure of scorn. The other term, on the contrary, has taken on a laudatory connotation: a sociable man, social services, social action. The term *social* or its numerous variants has been adopted by many political parties in Europe. In addition, if we note the prestige accorded to words which are similar due to the overtones with which they somewhat vaguely resonate – communism, collective, communal, the common good – then we have in a few words painted the picture. Whether one deplores this disjunction between the political and the social or celebrates it, it is an undeniable fact – confirmed moreover by the many who do not fulfill their duty to vote. One must ask what manner of collective life has evolved due to this remarkable semantic development. We all occasionally feel, with even a kind of anxiety at times, that the political superstructure – to use the words of Marx – corresponds less and less to the social infrastructure, and vice versa. [1]

---

1   See his *A Contribution to the Critique of Political Economy*, 1859.

That is the first phenomenon. There is a second immediately related to it. At the same time as politics is becoming increasingly suspect, considered as a last resort which people turn away from with hostility, we hear amid the silent rumbling of a society that is falling apart the quiet insinuating tread of a policy which as it is implemented exerts an increasing influence on us by means of the state as it imposes its dogmatism and at the same time its lackeys. We find ourselves in a paradoxical situation. On the one hand, society is in the process of collapsing and is groping to find new conditions in which it can exist. On the other hand, the politics of the state tighten their grip on it, and under the form of statism, take hold of human life in the measure that the state's political goals for society fail to find a way out in the midst of the chaos. Finally, people who instinctively reject the politicization of humanity are constrained to accept it since they lack the competence to do otherwise. We are witnessing the strangest series of arrangements and rearrangements there could be between the body politic and society, trying to reconnect to each other, less in order to unite than to devour each other. Everything is happening as though the mind, having abandoned the body which is now turned to dust, and finding itself without an identity, tries to get the body back in a great collective metempsychosis,[2] to transform it according to its image.

These two phenomena are relatively recent. Two hundred years ago, political science was the most valued of the practical sciences. This was the case in the age of Louis XIV, the Middle Ages, and antiquity. To give only one example, a chronicler of the thirteenth century, Brunetto Latini, wrote "Politics, that is the government of states, is the most noble and exalted science, and the most noble office

---

2   Transmigration of the soul into a new body.

on earth".[3] Up to the last great representative of the tradition inaugurated by Plato,[4] without a doubt Jean Bodin,[5] political science has always been considered as the crowning achievement of human life and as its most perfect earthly expression. "Man is by nature a political animal" Aristotle had said.[6] It is not unusual to find ancient, medieval, and Capetian[7] texts which call political science "divine". The myth recounted in *Protagoras* is symbolic in this regard.[8] Plato tells us in this work how Prometheus stole into the workshop of Vulcan and Minerva to steal the secret of fire and so provide man with all that was necessary for life. But man did not receive knowledge of political thought, because Jupiter had dominion over that. Prometheus was not able to enter the sanctuary of the king of the gods, the entrance to which was protected by fierce guards. And the continuation of the dialogue is even more significant, since Protagoras the sophist introduces a new Prometheus, happier and bolder, who, in the figure of Mercury, the god of economics, claims to teach all men about this science formerly hidden by the father of men and gods. Doesn't this old story have a surprisingly modern flavor?

Beginning in the eighteenth century, Voltaire did not hesitate to say, "Politics is nothing but the art of deliberately lying."[9] D'Alembert echoes this: "War is the art of destroying men, as politics is the art of deceiving them."[10]

---

3   C. 1220-1294, Florentine philosopher and statesman. The citation is from *Li livres dou tresor*, written in old French, 1260-1267.
4   See, for example, his *Republic* and *The Laws*.
5   1529/30-1596, French political philosopher and jurist who wrote on political theory.
6   *Politics*.
7   Referring to the French dynasty founded by Hugh Capet which ruled France from 987 to 1328.
8   In this work, one of Plato's dialogues, Socrates converses with the aged Protagoras, a notable sophist and philosopher.
9   *Annales de l'Empire depuis Charlemagne*, 1754.
10   Jean Le Rond d'Alembert, 1717-1783, French mathematician, physicist, philosopher, and music theorist. The citation is from *Mélange de litterature, d'histoire, et de philosophie*, 1753-1767. Writing from memory,

Since then, the protest against politics has intensified, to the point where there is no longer even one Machiavelli who is not able to take advantage of this in order to work his way to power. We know today, through bitter experience, that rival political parties, no matter what they stand for, continually rise up against each other to accuse each other of lying or betrayal, without worrying about how this affects the foundations of society, which are in a state of collapse until one party, seizing the power coveted by all either by a majority vote or totally different means, expels its enemies and sets out on the path to totalitarianism. Baudelaire had already described this in the nineteenth century with his wonderful poet's intuition:

> The poison of power weakening the despot
> And the people in love with the stupefying whip. [11]

How can we explain this twofold phenomenon which causes disruption to the point of violence between these opposing forces, these two perfectly complementary aspects of collective life, the political and the social? This seems impossible to us without putting forth the hypothesis, confirmed by history, of the constant potential in man for the diminishment of his vitality and of his ability to adapt to the ensemble of persons and things with which he has an immediate relationship, the whole of which constitutes society. Man then compensates for the lack of rootedness in his social life with theoretical edifices, the poisoned fruits of his disembodied mind, which give him the illusion of a life, a life with stability. The more that spontaneous social connections, necessitated by the presence of those near him, are weakened, the more political theory, elaborated in hothouse systems of thought, gains influence over him. Normally courses of action taken in common proceed from

---

De Corte attributes the words of Voltaire to d'Alembert and vice versa. This has been corrected here.

11 "Le voyage," *Fleurs du mal*, 1857. Charles Baudelaire, 1821–1867, French poet, essayist, and translator, considered the originator of symbolism.

the bottom up, taken up successively by groups connected to each other by the force that impels man to live in society, affecting the soul of the politics resulting from this organization. Yet when this vitality weakens, becomes enervated, and disappears, the process then proceeds inversely, from the top down, from the soul, now without a body, that sustains society with a political theory dedicated to create out of nothing an artificial community corresponding to it, reaching the isolated individual, lost in a sort of social no man's land, who must receive the imprint of this theory, always the same, in the depths of his being. This soul and this political theory do not arise from concrete man, tied by birth and vocation to a social milieu, since in their fundamental weakness they are incapable of enabling him to exist. They can be nothing but an emanation coming from man abstracted from all his basic social connections, a product deriving from ideation or from the character of a particular group, such as the bourgeoisie, the proletariat, or race. [12] By means of a system of thought or the character of a group, this disembodied spirit tries in some fashion to imbue all people with its unique schema. Thus in a world where social life is ravaged, there arises a political system separated from life which is always striving to connect with man in order to create for him a poor substitute for social life: a specifically bourgeois, plebeian, or ethnic society. The man who somehow or other lives in the midst of the debris of a vanished society finds himself henceforth alone in the presence of a political system. In the face of it he experiences the same fear or fascination that the believer has before his God. He flees before it to hole away, far from his kind, within a solitude which is either pleasure-seeking or scornful, or perhaps he unreflectively gathers together with others, without communing with them in a way befitting human beings, in the huge enterprise of a wholly politicized state.

---

12 Or from a pressure group. Footnote of De Corte's.

We can show the consequences of this political and social retrogression in another way. That the social pertains to the nature of vitality in life is a fact demonstrated by all of human history: social life, and personal, solid, lasting contacts with one's neighbor, do not come from the deliberations of men. Social relations have their origin, far beyond elaborations of the mind or technology, from the overflowing, almost unconscious generosity which is the very hallmark of life. We have forgotten, since Rousseau and his many revolutionary followers, this ingenuous freedom in social life, the origin of *living organisms*, which the art of politics formerly codified with devotion, with the realization that it was then only necessary to provide social life with some supplementary principles. We have been going in the opposite direction, substituting what is arbitrary for what is required for social vitality. Now what is the opposite of a dynamic course of action but ankylosis[13] and this terrible form of a decline in vitality which is striking the modern world and which Thibon[14] and I have called paralysis agitans?[15] The principal work of all the revolutions unleashed in Europe over the past several centuries has been, from our point of view, to undo all the relations which solidly unite people to each other in their families, trades and professions, regions, and countries, and to make politics into an absolute, developed by a form of thought with its own logic, in which the individual, reduced to an isolated cell, wandering in the desert of a society rendered sterile from top to bottom, must then be remodeled according to the pattern designed by the despots. Today's revolutions are no longer spectacular, violent

---

13   Stiffening and immobility of a joint due to fusion of the bones or inflammation of tissues of the joint or associated muscles.
14   Gustave Thibon, 1903-2001, French philosopher and poet known for the originality and spiritual depth of his writing. There are many similarities between Thibon's and De Corte's thought.
15   Parkinson's disease. For the use of this term by De Corte, see his *Descartes, philosophe de la modernité*. Hora Decima, 2022.

movements, similar to a cleansing fever that frees the social body from its refuse, but profound underground tremors in social structures in the process of collapse, which are then reconstructed according to a contrived political theory. There are no longer sudden spasmodic outbursts which evidence a healthy reaction in the social organism, but long-lasting illnesses similar to a progressive exhaustion which settles in permanently and becomes a chronic condition, if we might call it that, and carries a whole people down the path of decline. Let us remember here the colloidal theory of the cause of death developed by Auguste Lumière. [16] This theory could be transposed in its entirety to the social domain. Just as in a living organism death is provoked by the coagulation of colloidal elements in cells which are no longer able to respond to physical forces exerted on each other when these elements, joining together, agglomerate into clumps, as this expert in medicine says, similarly social death is apparent when there is a similar agglomeration outside the natural communities into which man must become integrated, either by birth, in his family; by his vocation, his profession or trade; or by virtue of his destiny in the history of his region or nation. People then come together with their equals outside of these communities, to die, along with them, in the nebulosity of political ideologies. Let us suppose – with bitter irony, because we have this spectacle before our eyes – there is a "society" whose members are separated from each other because they have lost their social vigor, the source of living communities. Let us imagine isolated individuals, each in an airtight compartment, inattentive to any reality shared in common whether relating to the world around them or to their history, or, on the other hand, united together in a purely negative manner, such as the proletariat, for example, because they are incapable of participating in

16   1862-1954, French engineer, inventor, and biologist. See his *Théorie colloïdale de la biologie et de la pathologie*, 1922.

one or another of these realities due to their economic situation. Let us picture this "society" – or rather this dis-society [17] – bereft of common customs which bind citizens to a moral order to which they willingly subordinate their individual interests and which becomes incarnate in their lives like a reflex reaction. To put it another way, let us look at a group that comes apart starting at the bottom, in its social substructures and its collective aspirations, and whose members driving this – the "elite" – no longer have the feeling of belonging to a whole, and withdraw within themselves, attracting towards themselves this or that remnant of the dismantled community.

It is evident that in such an atmosphere of the dissolution of the social structure, people can only manage to come together under two different rubrics: one, which I shall call the *political*, the artificial representation of a new "society" and of a new man, creating out of nothing a "community, at last harmonious" where the new man makes an effort to live; the other which I shall call the *economic*, where the material interests of classes with selfish desires, be they individuals or groups, are given free rein.

We are witnessing on the one hand a social dissolution to the benefit of politics and economics, and on the other hand a singular reversal of values. The political no longer emerges from society; it does not appear, like fruit from a tree, from the rootedness of man in a well-structured community. On the contrary it arises in various forms: doctrinal, technical, scientific, juridical, mythical, or based on sentiments verging on the passionate, but in every case as something apart from life, and which operates on the wounded social instincts of man from outside him, subjects them to itself and reworks them according to its pattern, using them to its

17   The concept of dis-society refers to the dissolution in modern civilization of two of the three essential functions of every society, contemplation and action, to the exclusive benefit of the third, making (*poesis*) [Greek for the act of making]. Footnote of De Corte's. See his *De la dissociété*, Rémi Perrin, 2002.

advantage, to the point where, with Machiavellian skill, it can refashion and unify them into something new and false. The separation throughout society between the political and the social automatically spawns politico-economic totalitarianism. We have before us the "great beast" which Plato spoke of, or Valéry's Sémiramis, whose genius at empire building marshalled together her enslaved people with their capabilities and formed them to become one with her:

> Stupid people, to whom my power enchains me,
> Alas! My very pride has need of your aid!
> And what would my heart do if it loved not this hatred
> Whose many-numbered head is so soft under my feet. [18]

It is moreover significant that the whole of European politics has gone in the direction of a socialism strictly geared to political, and not social, ends. This politicization of existence means that the inborn capabilities of a society to construct a life in common which normally spur people to action do not have enough strength to give rise to a political system suited to them. The disappearance of these abilities engenders an ersatz social politics the same way that the scarcity of sugar brings saccharine to the market.

But it would be an error to believe that this political "socialism" which has invaded the modern world is the only example of this process of the politicization of the human being. All "bourgeois" politics developed in the same anemic social climate is in turn radically infected. Only the superstructure is different here, with a false, devitalized concept of society, where under an artificial, lifeless surface is a swarm of private interests. It seems obvious that from a sclerotic conservatism to various forms of political "socialism" there is uninterrupted continuity: in one case as in the other, the same weakness of social vitality (which creates organic communities) leads to their arrival on the

---

18   Paul Valéry, *Air de Sémiramis* in *Album des vers anciens*, 1920. Semiramis was a legendary queen thought to be modeled after an Assyrian queen regent who attained great power.

scene. The humorist Alphonse Allais[19] emphasized this resemblance in a remarkable quatrain:

> One would like to keep all the injustices for himself,
> The other says it's his turn to enjoy them,
> The whites are reds who have arrived,
> And reds are whites who are on the way.[20]

One sees the same process of social devitalization and political rationalization at work at the level of the state. It is obvious that man is increasingly treated like a thing which the state manages and on whom it puts its label, "made in . . . ,"[21] using a technique borrowed from business practices, which certain countries have brought to the ultimate point of perfection. It is not difficult to discern the lack of any social substance in this political rationalization of human activity effected by the modern state. The person, devitalized, his human resources run dry, projects outside himself the neurosis that serves as his world, that fascinates him, horrifies him, and later completely absorbs him. Jung declares that life not lived engenders neurosis.[22] One could adapt the expression: social life not lived in its natural settings then produces the colossal neurosis which is the current condition. This condition is no longer the embodiment of something endowed with life, it is no longer a people politically organized within a structure arising from their social vitality: it has an a priori form, with no human content. The art of politics no longer contributes anything relevant here because, as history runs its long course, nature no longer has enough strength to express the

19   1854–1905, French journalist as well as a humorist whose style tends to absurdism.
20   The color red has been associated with the left since the red flag of the French Revolution. White, the color of the Bourbon dynasty, represents monarchism in France.
21   "made in" in English in original.
22   Jung wrote, "About a third of my cases are not suffering from any clinically definable neurosis, but from the senselessness and emptiness of their lives. I should not object if this were called the general neurosis of our age." *Practice of Psychotherapy* (1929–1941) in *Collected Works*, vol. 16.

political perfection adapted to man's native social dynamism and which culminates in the form of the state. The political order which is the state then becomes an abstract super-structure outside time, situated above the impoverished societal life which it transcends and tyrannically dominates. Politics thus shows itself sequestered from the social aspect of life because the social dimension is lacking in vitality.

We thus understand why politics has become an idol increasingly the object of scorn, or – and this amounts to the same thing – giving rise to the worse kinds of fanaticism. This is because politics which follows a particular theory in fashion shows itself incapable of keeping its promises. Man is then reduced to nothingness accompanied by a kind of unconscious despair. Two centuries after the fall of the Ancien Régime, we are still awaiting a new society which, thanks to politics, was supposed to arise from its ruins. Revolutions, through which politics strives to attain this goal, either through violence or legal means, end in failure one after the other. A form of politics separated from the person who is integrated into natural, living communities is incapable of giving rise to a social order. It is in its very existence a permanent contradiction because it is made for the "government of a commonwealth" and there no longer exist "commonwealths" to govern, but what Valéry calls "the multiplication of isolated individuals."[23] For a political order to overcome this contradiction, there is only one solution left to it: to take complete hold of man and refashion him. A policy which can be labeled anti-birth because it prevents a society from being born is unfailingly succeeded by a policy practicing artificial insemination. It is moreover enough to reflect on the inevitable consequence of the concept of the *homo politicus* abstracted from the social influence of natural communities: the only result can be an omnipotent state, ubiquitous, totalitarian, and in its sovereign nothingness remaking man.

---

23   *Variété 2*, 1930.

THE SOCIAL AND THE COLLECTIVE

The disjunction between the political and the social leads to the disappearance of the latter to the benefit of the collective. It is necessary to set the social and the collective in sharp contrast not only because the latter caricatures the former and because it is more difficult to distinguish a thing from its copy than its opposite, not only because they are often confused with each other, whether by the partisans of individual freedom who repudiate the collective and ignore the social, or by their opponents who absorb the social into the collective, but above all because establishing these distinctions gives us the key to a series of phenomena which bear on the syndrome of the moral crisis of civilization.

The social exists: family, village, city, parish, region... The collective does not exist, except in the imagination. The social exists in the measure that it is organic, since it brings together human beings who live in relationship to each other like organs within a body: thus the father, mother, children, or also, in the utter simplicity of the relations among themselves, the village blacksmith who patronizes his neighbor the butcher, who in turn shoes his horse at the blacksmith's. Where there are social interactions, society exists, and social relations are particularly robust when they convey human warmth: thus kinship of blood and spirit brings about a fuller social existence than a purely economic relationship governed by the mathematical law *do ut des*. [24] We note in addition that economic ties, by the very fact of their presence, can lead to more robust social relations. The collective, on the contrary, has no existence other than the representation of itself by an idea, or rather by a poor example of an idea. Where the vitality of social relations weakens, the idea of the collective automatically arises as a model destined to serve as a guide in a chaotic world of monads with no cohesiveness, where social exchanges are

---

24 Latin, I give so that you may give in return.

reduced to a minimum. But this model does not refer to anything real; beyond the image, there is nothing. It is really enough to think for a moment about the addition of one thing to another, adding then a third, and so on, to get an idea of collectivity. This operation is only carried out in the mind, and nowhere else. Then what results in reality is only an inorganic juxtaposition of multiple units with purely imaginary bonds introduced by abstract thought.

The consequences of this distinction are enormous. To make a collectivity seem as though it really exists, it is necessary to create imaginary relations and persuade individuals that these relations are real. This would be needed if it were only to provide a phantom government and to repress a turbulent outbreak of anarchy. Yet for the imaginary relations to appear to be real, the imagination must be cultivated to the detriment of thought: for the mind knows, from reflection and experience, that these relations are imaginary and nonexistent. It is not due to chance, but because of an internal necessity, that contemporary civilization witnesses the development of ways to destroy the bond between the mind and reality, by creating images via newspapers, the cinema, and radio, which, due to the high speed at which they are transmitted, kill reflection. In a collectivity all reflection is banished. For societal bonds to seem to be real, it is important to prevent any comparison between real and imaginary ties: the best means available is to suppress real relations, amputating them from the human beings who maintain them, by, for example, instituting obligatory military service, or restructuring the economy. The only thing left then is to transform the imagination into a sort of debased faith, into a *fides de non visis*, [25] conferring an invisible existence to the nonexistent. All collectivism is a religion, and thus an anti-religion; a Church, and thus an anti-Church.

25   The object of faith is what is not seen, St. Thomas Aquinas, *Summa theologiae*, I-II, q. 66, art. 6; see also Hebrews 11:1.

But how to give substance to these imaginary relationships? First of all, through words. An organic relationship
is maintained in silence. Moreover, the more profound it is
the more inexpressible it is. Speech itself endows the imaginary rapport with a kind of winged, ambiguous existence,
halfway between earth and the heavens. On the one hand,
it is turned towards the subject which utters it, and on the
other, towards the objects it designates with ordinary words.
The imaginary rapport benefits from this leap of a word
towards the signification of what is taken to be existent in
order to appear real.

For this reason, all collectivities surround themselves
with a multitude of people who disseminate their verbiage. We hear in them the voice of the party, class, race,
nation, people, the great wave of mutterings coming from
phantoms emerging from a thicket rustling with words.
It is quite curious to observe that no one expatiates like
this in true societies, while everyone expresses himself
in collectivities.

Why this flood of words, printed matter, and images
hostile to straightforward thought and immediate experience? The reason for this is clear. It is not good to stir up
the depths of man as that reveals the emptiness of their
verbiage. One runs the great risk of giving rise to what
is real. It is thus necessary to tickle people's ears, utter
platitudes, launch the imagination in only one direction
so that it can have the maximum effect. Never evoking
what is concrete, which is always dense with meaning,
but rather a uniform, superficial abstraction, is a simple
shortcut to engage in a collective meditation. A logician
analyzing imaginary relations will always find them very
widespread and very little understood. On the other hand,
the feeling of being engulfed within imaginary relationships confers on them a coercive power that makes them
seem real, like someone shipwrecked who imagines that the
ocean is suffocating him, when just one wave is crashing

over him. Whence the rule for every collectivity: take over a greater collectivity.

One last point, legislative or administrative directives are of powerful assistance in the birth of collectivities. For the law is the *law*, and has tremendous power, thanks to the police who are there to impose respect for it. It is enough to compare the ages where real societies still existed with our own times. What is more real than power? Where collectivities dominate, we inevitably discover an abundance of laws and regulations, a large police force, and a multitude of government bureaucrats.

This list is not at all exhaustive. We could add the demand for, that is, the necessity of, the existence of what does not yet exist, the vision of the future, not here but to come ("onward, towards a thousand years of happiness . . . "), the fetishism of science which defines what is real . . .

Another consequence: since imaginary relations only exist in the imagination, they will have their greatest efficacy through the most powerful imagination, the furthest from any organic relationship and reality, in short, through a form of thought as devoid of content as can be. This ideation is understood here as an instrument which acts on the person. Whence the need for an orchestra conductor at the head of the collectivity who can gather together all the disparate units of the group into a gigantic imaginary relationship. To do this he will inevitably be constrained to get hold of them at their lowest level, the level of their smallest common denominator. Every collectivity has a leveling effect, while every society raises up. Every perfect collectivity requires just one operator, as Goethe said, "One mind is enough for a thousand hands."[26] This requirement is especially urgent as weak imaginations need outside help to galvanize them. Moreover they love

---

26   1749–1832, German poet, playwright, novelist, and statesman. The citation is from *Faust*, Part 2, 1931. Part 1 recounts how Faust sold his soul to the devil; Part 2 focuses on psychology, history, politics, and philosophy.

to find themselves within a powerful imagination where their mediocrity is given free rein, like a second-rate poet held up as a brilliant model, or a schoolboy attempting romantic poetry – in times past – as a Hugo. [27] Ages like ours demand such operators: with manual labor such as it is currently, making the soul anemic, escape via the imagination is a form of deliverance. Thus the prudent head of a collectivity should expand the use of servile work as much as possible. To assure his triumph, he will use the techniques of conjuring up an imaginary enemy and the threat of war, infallible means of exciting the imagination; reversing policies abruptly, which has an exhausting effect on the collectivity; provoking an inferiority complex which awakens its contrary; using other Machiavellian means to divert thought from tracking down reality.

All these characteristics of current political "life" are rooted in the disappearance of the social to the benefit of the collective and in the moral crisis engendered by this reversal.

Here we have the great, paradoxical truth: the collective, the terrifying "great beast" of Plato, does not exist. And most people suffer and die for what does not exist. Only the "unbelievers" will be saved. As the poet chants with bitterness, "There is no god at the altar where I am the victim."[28]

THE PROBLEM OF DEMOCRACY

Before, however, pursuing our inquiry, let us clear up a misunderstanding regarding the process of democracy and the people in charge of their destiny. This is an apologia for the past which you are putting forth, we will be told by modern minds, anxious to belong to their times. We will first respond with Lacordaire: "Belonging to one's times is to be subjected to and convinced by the prejudices of the age in which one lives. The philosopher who refrains

---

27 Victor Hugo, 1802-1885, great French Romantic poet, novelist, and politician.
28 Gérard de Nerval, 1808-1855, French Romantic poet, from "Le Christ aux oliviers" in *Les Filles du feu*, 1854.

from engaging with current ideas in order to reflect on the fundamental conditions of the existence of human societies does not have these weaknesses. He says what seems to him just and true, without worrying about whether or not this runs counter to any prevailing prejudice."[29] We then respond that democracy is a form of government as viable as any other, provided that it arises from a living society. We merely remark that the current dis-society is in grave condition and that to recommend a form of treatment for a person with a fever does not mean making him go back to the age he was before contracting his illness. We consider that the political order strictly depends on the social order, and not the other way around (exactly like the soul, in the sense in which Aristotle referred to it, is "something belonging to the body,"[30]) and that thriving epochs in history implicitly adhered to this law. As soon as we ask the future for credit, we hold that this request for funds is fraudulent because it is not based on any consciousness of it or, a fortiori, on any reality. The only thing we can know, with the approximate certainty given to us, in the order of the concrete – and the political like the social is extremely concrete – is the past. All former democracies which were disorganized on the social level and merely political evolved in the direction of tyranny. We have only to look for the cause of this. For us, this cause is obvious: political democracy which is not founded on a prior solid social democracy, that is, on family, professional, community, and regional structures developed on a human scale, where people are in contact with and understand each other in an organic, concrete way, because all feel they are bound to a common destiny, such a political democracy, without a social foundation, is the death of a people. At this point, if we want to purge democracy of its evils and

---

29   Jean-Baptiste Henri-Dominique Lacordaire, 1802-1861, French Dominican known for his powerful homilies, *Oeuvres du R. P. Henri-Dominique Lacordaire*, vol. 2, *Conférences de Notre-Dame de Paris, 1835-36; 1843.*
30   See his *On the Soul.*

make it healthy again, we must effect the indispensable *sanatio a radice*[31] and, apart from politics, establish the social foundations of the regime which indeed appears to be that of our times. Between living socially and perishing politically, the choice of each person not blinded by the prejudices of an absurd age is already made.

THE PARADOX OF POLITICAL POWER

We live in an age when, in the most monstrous of paradoxes, the political power of the citizen is exactly equal to his social powerlessness. To understand this, we are advised to look at the sociological content of the axiom operative in the functioning of the contemporary state: all power comes from the nation. This slogan – like every slogan – is at once accurate and inaccurate. If we apply it to a well-organized nation founded on social structures adapted to its growth, which it created in the course of history, this axiom teaches us nothing: it expresses a normal process. Royalty in France, for example, arose specifically from the organic development of French society during a particular age: from the bosom of the nation came the monarchical institutions and royal power which corresponded with the aspirations of the people. Here all power issued from a well-structured society. We could say as much about the Swiss republic. The meaning of the axiom is quite different, however, when it is a matter of a society without internal organs, such as our society, which shows itself incapable of expressing itself on the political level because it no longer has any cohesiveness. A nation like this is constituted from a socially amorphous entity which is trying to achieve unity. In this case, the political power it has can only be immense since it is no longer tied to social elements which would limit it by connecting themselves to it, more or less like an acorn limits the growth of the oak to which it gives birth and prevents it from becoming that monstrous tree which, in old Nordic

---

31   Latin, healing at the root.

legends, engenders the world.[32] This political power is basically *demiurgical* in nature and greatly superior to the divine right of kings because it bears the burden of remaking society, never undertaken under the Ancien Régime. As a result, the more a citizen is deprived of a social structure enabling him to thrive, the more will he demand political power so that in this way he can attain to a substitute for social life. This is clearly shown in the evolution of voting rights towards nothing other than universal suffrage in an increasingly unstable society. Power then always comes from the nation, but there are nations and then there are nations. Born from a society where the Ancien Régime collapsed under the weight of its deficiencies, its social stagnation, the demise of the organic communities of the family, trades and professions, the town and the region, all necessary complements of the social life of man, a bourgeois political democracy which limited the vote to those who paid a certain tax was bound to turn into a universal democracy. Money in reality only constitutes a bond of the most fragile sort. As for the connection between the possession of money and the lack of money, it is superfluous to remark that there is none. The use of truly universal suffrage brings about in some way the disaggregation of the social body. We repeat, it is not universal suffrage which is the cause of this (universal suffrage, implicit or explicit, has always existed), but its grip on a decaying society, where political groups take the place of social groups, with an increasingly perfected method. Each isolated individual, without lived social relations with his equals, is then aggregated with other individuals, but not as a function of his role in a society which in reality no longer exists, but as a function of his political opinions about the "dis-society": when worst comes to worst, the citizen, displaced socially, no longer even tolerates the restraint coming from the existence of

32   Yggdrasil, a huge sacred tree connecting and nourishing all things. The death of the tree would result in the end of the world.

several parties, which neutralize each other in the exercise
of power, or from the presence of a body of representatives,
who impede him from having any direct power. He wills to
take his identity from the state itself, via the single party
system, with no intermediary. We are then in the presence
of a totalitarian dictatorship – quite different from ancient
tyranny – which wholly refashions the foundations and
form of society. All power comes from the nation, particularly the power to change the social nature of man.

We then have an illusion, a collective neurosis in which
every living relation among people is mummified forever.
The more politics becomes separated from a well-structured
society, the more it is in fact separated from the people
who seem to exercise power. The all-powerful nation is
immobilized: its gigantic wings prevent it from walking.

POLITICAL ALIENATION

In the state of "dis-society", public opinion can only
reestablish social bonds by going back to a preconceived
system, outside the indeterminate social substance to which
it is applied, more or less as an engineer builds a piece of
machinery according to a preliminary blueprint where the
design is imposed to the smallest detail onto an amorphous
material, ready to be configured accordingly. Public opinion
can only take into account social elements which are still
viable by living off them as an external parasite and utilizing
their vulnerability in order to get across its reading of events.
The people, reduced to a kind of fluid shapelessness, thus see
the political power they hold as something which has become
external to themselves, imposing itself on them through the
will of a transcendent despotic state. The result is the true
political alienation of man, which Marx has described on
the economic level. For the more the people are deprived of
their social character and natural communities, the more
they lack internal organs of expression. What has been
called, somewhat humorously, "the coming of the masses

in history" is the tragedy of peoples foundering amid the disorganization and passivity characteristic of all masses. One will no doubt say that the people only delegate their power to proxies, whose action they control and who are always subject to recall. This is to ignore the common psychological principle that one only gives what one has: without social vitality the people are incapable of expressing themselves in society. Their representation will be merely political. Now political representatives will by this very fact be separated from the people, conceived of as a society which must be built. What is more, the representatives will experience the constant temptation, verified by contemporary history, to emphasize the transcendence of the state, where they are at the controls, as required by their very position: to effect the social reform instinctively desired by the people, the state must hold unlimited power over them. Thus the more those in charge want the "good" of the people, even with sincerity, the more they are called to treat them as a demiurge treats the world or the sculptor the malleable material of his work.

The assimilation of the people to the political power of the state, without the social counterweights which are indispensable, thus engenders a paradoxical situation, all of whose effects we experience in Europe: the political power of the state becomes the only active element in the nation, which is considered to have a passive role, since the people are constrained, by reason of their social deficiency, to divide into a politically active element and a social passive element. The people, deprived of their social character and politicized, have settled into the pathological condition of schizophrenia, which the poet has described:

> I am the wound and the knife!
> I am the limbs and the rack!
> I am the slap and the cheek!
> Both victim and executioner![33]

---

[33] Charles Baudelaire, "L'Héautontimorouménos" (Greek, "one's own executioner"), *Fleurs du mal*, 1857.

Europe is in a sickly state which it can only escape from through the reorganization of people into natural communities or through death.

THE SOLITUDE OF THE STATE

This has inevitable consequences, which turn into a vicious circle. In order to reduce the distance separating it from the people, the state is compelled to undertake a twofold enterprise which accentuates its overarching solitude even more.

On the one hand, it creates a bond with the people through all the strategies of propaganda and in particular through the promotion of a "mystique". In this sense, and contrary to the expression of Péguy,[34] we can say that politics degenerates into "mysticism". However, the precise character of this mysticism is to take away from the people the rudimentary political control they have and which makes them a danger to the state, a threat the more constant the greater is their social discontent. Thanks to this "mystique", the people are welded, so to speak, to the state or to the party which is aspiring to power in the state or which already possesses it just as iron, inert, adheres to a magnet. Political mysticism, like religious mysticism, produces ecstasy, the dissolution of the personality, not into someone within me who could be more myself than I am, as in the experience of the divine, but into the impersonal collective of the state or party. It is superfluous to add that the loss of personality is the very definition of slavery and that such a mystique is in reality a deception which makes the "sovereign" people slaves.

On the other hand, the state connects itself to the people by actions only apparently directed towards the social: the corporative organization,[35] for example, or the national-

---

34 "Everything begins with mysticism and ends in politics," *Notre jeunesse*, 1910.
35 Pius XI in *Quadragesimo Anno*, 1937, upholds the general notion of a corporative society built on Christian foundations, where corporations

ization of the means of production. Yet these moves are actually purely political, and only exacerbate the chronic state of affairs. Since it obeys a dialectic going from the top down, proceeding from the political power and going down to the underlying levels of society which it is attempting to reorganize socially, it gives birth to another kind of community, unheard of in history, where all movement and life, far from springing from man, are generated in him by the state. Thus an artificial society makes its appearance, born of political hypertrophy and the social devitalization of the citizen, where man's function is mechanical, like one gear engaging with another. Politics separated from the social becomes degraded here, in the end, into a strategy which takes away from citizens the last remains of their power. The two principles of politics, transformed into mysticism and state interventionism, will then be required to work together so well that we can formulate the following law: *In an atmosphere of tension between the political and the social, the closer the state comes to the people, the more their actual power passes away.* No one has been closer to the people than Napoleon, Lenin, or Hitler, who were the first to understand the character of our age, desocialized and politicized to an extreme degree; the states which they established possessed, in effect, all the power.

In democracies with multiple parties where the foundation is weakening the phenomenon is the same: it merely occurs in stages. Each party constitutes a kind of autonomous state with its leadership of "mystics" and technical staff, where the same process is mirrored. Recent history clearly shows, moreover, that the party which is in solidarity with the *socially disinherited* element of the people governs in a mechanical way as it sees fit.

---

with representatives of both labor and management work together for their mutual benefit and that of society. Under Mussolini, corporative organizations involved state recognition of labor unions, which alone could make labor contracts, yet were ultimately under the control of state authorities.

AN ECONOMIC LEVIATHAN[36]

The politicization of a citizen who no longer feels the concrete presence of bonds uniting him to the state contributes to the destruction of the last social ties that might unconsciously remain in him. Obsessed by the vision of a future heralded as imminent, but caught up in the gyrations of politics which take away his social personhood, the citizen cuts away the last moorings by which he is still connected to a living collectivity. He becomes, in the strict sense of the word, a partisan. Nothing matters to him now in comparison with what he passionately covets, neither family, friends, work, nation, religion. He is entirely taken up by the political machine. It is then that he finds himself confronted with social emptiness, in which he must henceforth live.

What can he do? How can he direct his life? For in the disappearance of his social world and the natural communities around him, he has lost everything, and is left with only his material and physiological needs: eating, drinking, sleeping, relaxing . . . , accompanied by the political perspective of a better society, which captivates him. Neither of these ill-defined drives operative in him would be content with anarchy. A lack of organization only makes these needs more intense. The desocialized man, expelled from his social contexts, which supported him and which were adaptable since they were living, yearns for rigid political structures, which enable him to live in the material sense. He wants rigid regulations, cast in concrete, terribly harsh if necessary, which would ensure his survival. At this stage the political ideology will be nothing other than a rigorous mechanism thanks to which the new society is founded on

---

36   Thomas Hobbes, 1588-1679, English philosopher best known for *Leviathan* (1651), which upholds the need for an absolute central authority in the state, termed a Leviathan. Individuals accept a social contract ceding power to the government in return for protection from civil disruption and of property. Hobbes terms the state an artificial man, artificial because not occurring in nature but created by the people in their image.

a purely economic basis. Society has then become a huge factory where man draws his sustenance, on the condition that he serve in its ranks, which have been methodically established: *the great Leviathan* of Hobbes has appeared, *which is but an artificial man.*[37] All the features of politics separated from the social follow from this situation.

POLITICAL ORTHODOXY

The chief of these characteristics – and the one that goes the most unnoticed – is inner consistency. Politics develops for itself and into itself, as a function of its own content. Political truth in this sense follows a general direction. It can perhaps allow certain deviations, sometimes even dramatic reversals, but only regarding details: its direction remains invariably the same. Moreover, it only shifts where it encounters social resistance to its influence; it takes this into account, not to mine its content and promote its development, but to crush it. Any other attitude is forbidden to politics: *detached from society because society is devitalized and unable to give rise to a political system suited to it, politics can only be sustained by itself, in the meshing together of its own cogwheels,* as much from the ideological as from the practical point of view. Politics thus becomes a *Weltanschauung,* and even a religion. In this regard it is noteworthy that politics has become doctrinal and even doctrinaire in contemporary "society": the more visible the faults in the structure of society are, the more rigid and without fissure the political system is. Thus an orthodoxy develops which tends not only to expel the heretic and independent-minded, but to attain that union without love, which, according to Augustin Cochin, is the very definition of hate,[38] and which groups people together less according to their living relationship than because of their

---

37   Italicized words are in English in the original.
38   1876-1916 (killed in World War I), French historian of the French Revolution, which he examined from a sociological perspective. See his "Réflexion," 1909, in *La Révolution et la libre-pensée,* 1924.

lifeless standardized ideas. As a result, the human being, plunged into this noxious environment, defines himself by comparing and contrasting himself with his fellow man, as occurs with everything that is material, without life: it is only from the perspective of life that an organic relationship is found. This is why citizens grouped in this way into political parties, whose natural roots, common to all humans, are cut off, can only be implacably opposed to each other. The parties here do not involve secondary and complementary distinctions, with a common substructure similar to life, shared with the organs of the same body, but primary, antagonistic compartmentalizations into which the whole person is placed, setting him against his neighbor.

What is called class struggle is, from this point of view, only the predictable result of a humanity defined by its economic needs on the one hand, and by its political opinions on the other, to the exclusion of the strictly social factor having to do with natural communities.

A NEW FORM OF SOPHISTRY

Furthermore, speculative thought, taken in its twofold meaning of doctrinaire and economic, contributes to the increase of political power cut off from its social roots. Where there is an order which is truly social, there is an infinite complexity of elements which interpenetrate each other, a mass of factors adapted to the community in a way which is invisible because they are lived and integrated into daily activities. Speculative thought is unaware of them, or if they still have some substance, eliminates them as irrational, since it operates in a sovereign way only on what is inert, on the abstract residue of life, *in vitro*.

The triumph of ideological thought is its standardized consistency, similar to an algebraic formula, which dispenses it from taking into consideration what is concrete and living. In antiquity ideological thought under the guise of philosophy was associated with tyranny, while today it has been placed under the rubric of science, the ally of an effective dictatorship or the embryonic form of it, which we are now experiencing. This ideology is everywhere in the process of substituting its own laws, appropriate for inert material, for the "illogical" surges of life immanent in every well-organized society. The scientific and the political have recourse to each other as soon as society goes from a living to an inorganic state, and from a phase endowed with life to one where everything is reduced to the physical. Politics has need of science in the measure to which it seeks to discover the laws governing the disaggregated atomistic elements which people have turned into and to dominate them completely.

A complete methodology for psychological manipulation has thus been put at the service of the transcendent state. Balzac had a premonition of this when he wrote, "to skillfully make use of the passions of men and women as springs which one sets in motion, to set in place the gears of this big machine which we term a government, and to be pleased to take hold of the most unconquerable emotions and use them as release mechanisms that one enjoys monitoring, isn't this to create, and like God, to put oneself at the center of the universe?"[39] Science, in turn, has need of such a political system to achieve its universal dream of a methodical order. We see the ultimate in this reciprocal attraction in the societal machine described by Huxley in *Brave New World* whose administrators are lucid, unfeeling technicians.

It is pointless to add how this interpenetration contributed to the absolute transcendence of politics with regard to the social and to the elimination of the last affective bonds which bring people together. Some very clear examples of this alliance between positivism and politics disengaged from people are supplied by the relations between Diderot

---

39 *Les Chouans*, 1829.

and Catherine the Great,[40] Voltaire and Frederick II,[41] Auguste Comte and Czar Nicholas.[42]

Why is the contemporary intellectual becoming increasingly involved in politics? Why is politics always looking for support from positive science? A new form of sophistry, similar to the one denounced by Plato, is today rapidly taking shape, which goes from statistics conceived as an instrument for surveying opinions to nuclear physics presented as a way to dominate the planet, and including medicine designated as social, and what Thibaudet calls the "republic of professors."[43] It is not difficult to establish the reason for this noxious influence. The distinctive feature of positive science is to *objectify* the world, just as the characteristic trait of modern politics is to *objectify* man.

For the scientist the world is an ensemble of strictly *objective* phenomena, in which he is in no way involved personally: a formulaic schema accompanies each of his explanations. There is no prior link between the thinking of the scientist and the object which he studies. Existence as well is devoid of meaning for him: he acts towards beings as though they did not exist, as though a being were only a series of antecedents and consequences, as though he

---

40 Denis Diderot, 1713-1784, French philosopher of the Enlightenment. Catherine the Great, 1729-1796; reigned 1762-1796 as a despot, though inspired by the philosophy of the Enlightenment, which inspired her to found universities and theaters, and to improve health care. Catherine rescued Diderot from his financial woes by bringing him to Russia, buying his library, and employing him to take care of it.

41 Voltaire, 1694-1778, French historian and philosopher of the Enlightenment. Frederick the Great, 1712-1786, king of Prussia, reigning 1740-1786, who believed in enlightened absolutism. The two maintained a long-lasting correspondence, in spite of their differences, Voltaire in his defense of civil liberty criticizing the king.

42 Auguste Comte, 1798-1857, French philosopher, the founder of the doctrine of positivism. He contributed to the development of sociology. Nicholas I, 1796-1855, autocratic emperor of Russia, 1825-1857. Comte wrote to the czar, asking him to adopt positivism and a humanistic religion, an appeal which bore no fruit.

43 Albert Thibaudet, 1874-1936, French literary critic and professor. He applied the term "republic of professors" to the Third French Republic (1870-1940) in his *La République des professeurs*, 1927.

himself, in his role as a scientist, did not exist, save as an impartial spectator of a mere succession of events to be analyzed. Before the text of the universe, the scientist acts like a grammarian who only studies linguistic signs without delving into what is actually signified. As Meyerson has shown,[44] the positivist conception of science is inspired by a more profound tendency, proper to human reason which has broken off its rapport with what is real. Theories developed by the modern scientist to explain phenomena and enclose them within a network of laws all tend to base the discovery of their actual causes on a process of identification: to explain an effect is to identify it with its cause, to reduce the effect to its cause; this is to bring unity to diversity, and homogeneity to heterogeneity. Taken to its limit, scientific explanation eliminates quality, time, and plurality to the benefit of pure monism, which could be formulated in this way: everything is only this or that — matter, space, reasoning, logic . . . —from which the universe can inevitably be deduced. Just as someone perched on a bluff watches the varied landscape, which he is no longer part of, dissolve into a uniform mass, so the vision of what is real for the scientist, from the lofty perspective of his science, ends up as something invariable which imposes its peremptory features on the multiplicity of beings. But in fact this cosmogony is only a dream introduced by rational thought into reality in order to undo it since it is resistant to a comprehensive explanation: "Rational thought has only one way of explaining what does not proceed from itself, which is to reduce it to nothing."[45] Thus, as Nietzsche portended, the modern scientist is condemned to nihilism.[46] He can only deny the existence of what exists since separating himself from it

---

44   Émile Meyerson believed that analytic thought was the death of thought. See his *De l'explication dans les sciences*, 1921.

45   Meyerson, see the volume referenced above.

46   In *The Gay Science*, 1882, Nietzsche argues against classical rationalism and scientific positivism.

causes his death, just as a limb amputated from the body is deprived of life.

The comparison between social structures and contemporary politics, separated from the social, is striking. Modern political man is almost without a relationship to social reality, in which he should take part by reason of his birth, vocation, and destiny in history. His actions are carried out keeping in mind the electoral process and its impact. With the exception of life at home, where he has a role, one can say that there is probably no bond between him and others, except as occasioned by superficial contact every now and then. The social existence of the human being in natural communities has no significance for him: when he encounters them, he behaves as though they did not exist, as though he himself had no social existence, as though he were a scribe documenting an inorganic "will of the people". Face to face with social reality, he behaves for his part like a lexicographer who disregards syntax. Yet this is only the most superficial characteristic of his attitude. In fact, his action is directed by a more profound philosophy, still unconscious and required by his original role of *homo politicus*, denuded of social sensitivity. The utter diversity of which he is a representative would remain anarchic if it were not gathered into the unity of a compact whole. The multiplicity of persons which he represents has become in his eyes a kind of single gigantic individual: the people, the party, a class, a language . . . which takes the place of an organic, diverse society. Taken to its limit, this homogeneous grouping is itself reduced to one concept of man: man is his mind, man is matter, man is a producer, man is a consumer . . . As a result of this concept of man, there comes into play a sort of deduction about social life parallel to that made by the scientist. Society has to be this or that, can only be this or that; it is a homogeneous mass which will submit to the imprint of the initial concept as its dialectical process proceeds from top down. Everything outside this concept will be pitilessly eliminated: "Rational thought has only one way of explaining what does not proceed from itself, which it to reduce to nothing."[47]

To see that here there is a new form of sophistry which transposes on to the framework of contemporary civilization the same basic pattern of the ancient form, it is enough to read the dialogues of Plato to be convinced. The sophist like the modern scientist is the technician of politics, indifferent to the concrete good and evil resulting from the deployment of his strategies: the presence of this good and evil can only be detected through participation in social life. The techniques are self-justified, due to their success, which is the conquest of power, which in turn assures their absolute efficacy. Little does it matter if man is reduced to the state of a robot: politics has come full circle and, detaching itself from the social to bind itself to science, it becomes its own end. Thanks to appropriate techniques, learned from science, everything begins with politics and ends with it. For this reason Plato continually associates sophistry and tyranny with a policy that fluctuates between terror and the satisfaction of the most material pleasures of the citizen. Science in the hands of politicians has become an instrument of universal fear and earthly pleasures: one and the other replace the vanished natural society where man freely flourished through participation in the very community to which he had been destined.

A MATERIALISTIC ORIENTATION OF LIFE

Such politics will inevitably take on an increasingly materialistic cast. Let us briefly look at the trajectory politics has taken since European society has entered into decline.

It is clear that a society which is becoming undone is freed from all kinds of constraints which intervene in daily social life. Within the framework of a social order, people function freely but with a reciprocal interdependence. In a

---

47 Meyerson, *La déduction relativiste*, 1925.

living society, liberty is never the antithesis of social bonds, to which it is the true complement. Thus sound business practices among tradesmen and craftsmen who experience a mutual dependence engender in them a feeling of liberty, ease, familiarity, pleasure in one's work, and an absence of constraints, something unknown in a huge factory with no internal cohesion. Similarly an affectionate connection to the corner of the earth where they were born, without their choice, creates in the citizens of a region a taste for liberty which the rootless man will never feel. Liberty is here the crown and flowering of a lived need for the social. On the other hand, as soon as social bonds dissolve in a society in the throes of death, liberty is cast out of the sphere of communion and interdependence: it becomes abstract, theoretical, in other words, nonexistent, and degenerates into automatism, servitude, and death. Thus the worker who is no longer connected to his employer and works in a business where he is only an element interchangeable with others can only be called free by the classical liberal economy or by the state which suppresses employers' authority. But the iron-clad rule of the market, in effect in his place of work, and the bureaucratic tyranny of the state weigh on him with their full force. Thus the employer separated from the worker because he no longer shares with him the common lot of the business in which they are associated can call himself free: he is in fact the slave of capital.

As Chesterton humorously remarks, in opposition to Gide,[48] " . . . the home is the only place of liberty. Nay, it is the only place of anarchy. It is the only place on earth where a man can alter arrangements suddenly, make an experiment, or indulge a whim. Everywhere else he goes he must accept the strict rules of the shop, inn, club, or museum that he happens to enter. He can eat his meals

---

48   André Gide, 1869-1951, French novelist, dramatist, essayist, and translator, awarded the Nobel Prize for literature in 1947. He proposed a new ethics to replace traditional morality.

on the floor in his own house if he likes ... For a plain, hardworking man, the home is not the one tame place in the world of adventure. It is the one wild place in the world of rules and set tasks. The home is the one place where he can put the carpet on the ceiling or the slates on the floor if he wants to. When a man spends every night staggering from bar to bar or from music hall to music hall, we can say that he is living an irregular life. But he is not; he is living a highly regular life, under the dull, and often oppressive, laws of such places."[49] However, the most typical example here is undoubtedly the proletariat: the liberty he seems to enjoy, granted him by the political system, is nothing but an empty word, because he does not form part of any living society. This is why proletarianized societies are ready-made prey for totalitarianism.

All promotion of the ideal of liberty in a society which is falling apart ends with inflated political power and authoritarianism in its most machine-like form. *Social needs, denied for those at the bottom, are despotically reconstituted at the top via the machinery of the state; liberty is only the common term for servitude.*

From then on what was originally idealism inevitably turns into materialism: when the soul which they have in common no longer holds together the different organs of the body, one must have recourse to chemistry by means of medications. Politics is then constrained by an imperious necessity, since man expelled from his social context sees at the same time that his material stability is compromised. Thus the ideology of liberty engenders ideological materialism, which impels man to consider everything only in view of production, consumption, and the distribution of earthly goods. In antiquity, this came in the form of *panem et circenses*. In the state the world is in today, it comes under the more complex form of obsession with the

---

49   From "No Place Like Home" in *What's Wrong with the World*, 1910.

economic. The social classes, deeply divided among and between themselves, fight over the ownership of the means of production in order to shore up their faltering security. The ideal of liberty, denuded of all social obligations and the restraints of healthy ethics which flow, like life-giving blood, through the foundational communities into which man must be integrated in order to live as a human being, is transformed into the ideal of material security. Political power, be it in a natural or unnatural form, legitimate or illegitimate, is made to bring about order, and thus can only be extended. The rupture of organic social relations under the pressure of the ideology of liberty must also lead, amid the growing lack of stability, to political power setting itself up as the universal guarantor of human life and its material requirements. Poor and rich are united here: the first because they have nothing, the second because they are afraid of losing their possessions in the hazardous fluctuations which disorder brings with it. Political power is thus anchored in the plebeians and the lowest strata of society, and makes an alliance with the *beati possidentes*. [50] If it is Machiavellian, it engages in cold-blooded double-dealing to increase its power. In spite of his diatribes against "pluto-democracies", Hitler did not act otherwise in Germany. The very dialectic of power without roots obliged him to do this, and the secret of recruiting praetorians[51] consisted merely in removing SS candidates from their families, regions, and all their primary social communities, and isolating them within the political system.

THE BUREAUCRATIZATION OF EXISTENCE

On the other hand, there is a need for specialists to accomplish tasks large and small in order to ensure order within the hierarchy and to unravel the complications of intertwined material interests. Political power becomes

---

50 Latin, the blessed ones who have.
51 Bodyguards of Roman emperors.

bureaucratized with a disconcerting rapidity. It is transformed into a dictatorship of administrative technicians
who, at the controls of political and economic power, direct
from the top down all of human life from the brain to the
entrails; a living heart no longer exists in society, but a
watch-like mechanism. Isolated within their "science", they
have no more contact with "society", except to transmit
their orders to it. Moreover, the members of the "society",
hypnotized by their yearning for security or material advantage, give all their support to the political powers in return
for forming part of the "protected sector" of the bureaucracy.
The disjunction between the political and the social is then
consummated. Though the political powers are far from
arising from a well-organized, living nation, the nation in
its totality depends on this ensemble of powers within the
state. We have before us an artificial society, completely
reconstructed, turned upside down, which will "normally"
be identified with the most artificial social groups: the
police and military. Society becomes militarized from every
point of view. Taken to the limit, isolated political power,
where natural communities no longer have any role, then
results in total war, since it cannot tolerate any obstacle in
its path, any authority other than its own. The experience
of Hitler, like that of the Jacobins[52] and to a lesser extent
Napoleon, is sufficiently eloquent. These leaders came
from a political democracy which was not first organized
into a social democracy.

This divorce between the political and social is, by all evidence, a product of what we have elsewhere called the
devitalization of man: weakened, agitated, retaining none
of his human substance, the man of today has proved to be
incapable of producing a living society which might, with
only the beating of its heart, infuse lifeblood into politics

---

52   Radicals who planned the French Revolution.

and economics, the brain and entrails of society. The society of today is afflicted with heart disease and arterial sclerosis. An illness like this can only be cured over time.

If we judiciously sound the future, we perceive three possible directions in which society could evolve:

1. The process which we have just described, already off to a good start in several countries of Europe, will continue implacably. This will be the *finis Europae*,[53] the end of the moral order in Europe foreseen by Bonald.[54] The small Hellenic peninsula, which in ancient civilization played a role similar to that taken on by Europe for more than a thousand years, and the vast Roman empire, ended in that way. Europe enters into history as a dust-covered, fragile mummy.

2. Europe will be invaded by foreign peoples who, as in the age of barbarians, enjoy a social vitality whose political maturation has not yet been achieved. Only Russia and Asia find themselves in this situation, as far as we can tell. Yet Russia herself has already received a massive dose of the European virus. It is possible, even probable, that she will get rid of it. Nevertheless, this reaction, characteristic of human life, will be drawn out, especially after international and civil wars which will only widen the gap between the political and the social and will exacerbate still more the conflict between them.

3. Europe has hit bottom and will climb back up. We are at the low point of the curve which outlines the long crisis which has been weakening us for more than two centuries: the society which neither the politics of the French Revolution nor any later political system has given us will, slowly at first, reconstitute itself, more or less as Christian society was formed during the "night" of the early Middle Ages. Europe is like a sick person who refuses to swallow the "salvific" potions which doctors have prescribed for it, from specialists to charlatans, and all those in between,

---

53   Latin, end of Europe.
54   Louis de Bonald, 1754–1840, French philosopher and politician who opposed the principles of the Enlightenment and French Revolution. His extensive writings also addressed the traditional family and the natural laws of the social order.

and who trusts in nature up to the last gasp of the life which animates him: *natura medicatrix*. [55] Europe has had enough of all the quacks of the left or right, parlimentarians or anti-parlimentarians, who have chosen it as a guinea pig for their experiments. Europe will depoliticize and resocialize itself.

What can we say?

This means that the ruling power – which always remains, since anarchy is temporary – becomes clairvoyant and knows how to establish a clear distinction between the political and the social, to better unite them. If we may be permitted to make a comparison, Europe is like a fractured limb that has healed in the wrong position, and which must be broken again to ensure proper alignment and thus the ability to walk and to engage in work normally. Europe is lost if: the regnant power insists on claiming that society must be this particular thing, then after an upheaval which replaces it, on proclaiming that society must be that other thing; it forges a compromise between these two affirmations, becomes rigid in its will to transform society radically, or to let society become infected with the political poison with which the power itself has contaminated the people. It is important for the government to keep faithful vigilance over the seeds of a social life eager to be reborn and over natural communities, from which man frees himself only to consign himself to the grave, and to remove anything hindering the growth of these seeds. But let us not expect too much clear-sightedness from the state: the remaking of a modern society organized at last around its natural communities depends on us, on our daily activities in the bosom of our families, businesses, labor unions, towns, and villages, through continually exercising the social functions of which we are capable. We will only infuse lifeblood into an anemic society if we are brimming over with vitality.

---

55 Latin, the healing power of nature.

Such a task is straightforward, yet enormous. It demands:

1. *The extinction of the myth of equality which creates an insur-mountable divide between the social and the political.* The social is never egalitarian, since it is essentially the union of a variety of organs, of members brought together and oriented to a common destiny.

2. The *participation* of all levels of the social hierarchy into one body in society, just like the organs of a living body. (The abdication of responsibility and the inertia of the "elites" are in this regard just a product of their lack of rootedness in society.)

3. The establishment of relatively small social cells where the feeling of "we" can be lived and is within man's reach by means of proximity and meaningful social exchanges. As Chesterton has said, "For a big state, the most glorious hope consists in envisioning its happy, skillful transformation into a small state."[56]

This task requires, in addition to time, patience, customs and traditions, which allow man to re-create for himself roots and standards of behavior within his social milieu, and which permit members of the elite to bring life to the heart of the community that they represent. It assumes finding a solution to the great drama of industrial civilization, anchored by capitalism and organized according to the principles of statism, where individuals get lost in the mass of men, where money and bureaucratic decrees abolish all viable relations, where property loses its character of being of social benefit and becomes theft which profits parasitic individuals, a caste of bureaucrats, or a national mysticism. This effort postulates the reintegration into the round of social life of the vast lumpen-proletariat[57] brought into being by the primacy of money

---

56   Throughout his work, Chesterton defends the superiority of what is small versus what is large. See, for example, "On Certain Modern Writers and the Institution of the Family" in *Heretics* (1905).

57   A German term coined by Marx and Engels referring to the proletariat underclass, including the chronically unemployed, the homeless, and criminals.

over work and whom the political state has made into a defined class everywhere.

More generally, the task calls for the rapprochement of traditionalism and socialism, having rid themselves of their political superstructures of whatever stripe. People will say that such an undertaking is reactionary. We reply that being reactionary means for us, as dictated by good sense, the will to impose on social problems a retrograde political solution, or one which keeps the status quo, or — at best — progresses towards a politics of domination. The social question is on the contrary merely social; its end is the achievement of a living unity in a living diversity and not the possession of power.

If political democracy does not understand this truth of utmost importance, if it does not see that its guarantor is a people well-organized socially, then it is already at the reactionary and tyrannical impasse where nonviable governments fail. It then prepares along with its own ruin that of society and civilization.

CHAPTER 3
Technology and Collectivism

TECHNOLOGY IS THE IDEAL OF CON-
temporary civilization. Its goal is to effect the
liberation of man with regard to nature and all
other domains, religious, social, political, aesthetic, psycho-
physiological . . . In each of these areas, a form of applied
science is implemented to achieve this goal. Of all these
converging ways of freeing man from nature and subjugating it, modern economics serves as the most visible icon:
embodied in spectacular forms of automation, particularly
seen in the machines that come between man and nature, its
techniques have become Techniques par excellence, around
which all the others revolve. Whether we like it or not,
contemporary man follows a path in line with the one
delineated by Karl Marx, where economic infrastructures
control all the superstructures. This evolution seems to be
inevitable. Certain Christians, like the Marxists of strict
observance, have seen in the evils engendered by technology
only a "crisis of growth" which must precede the trans-
figuration of man . . . From the equation set up between
technology, economics, domination of the world, and the
liberation of man, something unknown has to arise: the
new man. But it is important to ask ourselves: what man?

Let us say it right from the start: it is not a matter here
of a value judgment about technology. It has always existed,
and always will. As soon as we define it as the ensemble of
processes employed by artisans and tradesmen, we perceive
the permanent need for it: it is the natural extension of
the intellect and hands, and without it, man would find

himself as deprived as an animal cut off from its instincts. Yet it is of the essence of technology to be contentless: it is merely a channel for human activity. Everything depends on its content, everything depends on the outcome to which it leads. Technology can serve as a vehicle for good or evil, being or non-being, inspired or impoverished thought, and can be oriented towards the heights or the depths. Technology only derives meaning from its origin and from its end.

These concepts are elementary. An important consequence follows from them: technology should be adapted to man and not man to technology. A violinist could use a bow two feet long, but the most noble musical inspiration could not find expression on an outsized instrument. In this case it stagnates, becomes distorted, and ends up by disappearing. There is nothing at the mouth of the stream since there is no longer anything at the source, for want of an appropriate intermediary. What kind of man, then, is at the origin of modern technology? It suffices to look into it to find out.

WHY TECHNOLOGY IS COLLECTIVE IN NATURE

The observer is immediately struck by the collective character of current technology: in all activities having to do with the transformation of matter, the phenomenon has taken on an unprecedented breadth. Moreover, the domain of the intellect is not an exception: perhaps it is even more subtly affected. Without mentioning research departments or boards of directors, which are the norm in contemporary economics, it is enough to consider the structure of science today: no single mind can encompass it in its entirety. There is no form of technology, no applied science, which does not require the collaboration of a multitude of specialists.

This process is well-known, but its cause less so. Generally it is attributed to an imperious necessity: the division of labor, required by the complexity of tasks required by a civilization which is growing, extending its domain, and exalting itself. This example reminds us of Molière: it is like the *virtus dormitiva* of opium. [1] One sees another comparison in the increasing diversity in organisms as they are higher up in the hierarchy of life: there is no specialization within the amoeba, we are told, while there is in an animal which has further evolved. The determinism associated with progress requires this. So it is in contemporary civilization, more developed, more advanced than any which have gone before it.

Of course, specialization in the function of biological organs cannot be denied. Yet it is always accompanied by a unity, itself organic as well, increasingly intensified and pronounced. While one can divide an animalcule, we cannot destroy the biological unity of a more complex animal without putting it in danger of death. The kidneys do not perform the same function as the heart, but their mutual union is so powerful that, in spite of their specialized function, if one of them becomes weak, the other comes to its aid to the point of exhausting itself. Indeed, the experience of history gives undeniable witness to this: technical specialization and the collectivism which accompanies it always appear at the moment when the unity among men becomes more precarious, less organic. Technical skills became more specialized as the Greek state was collapsing. An extreme division of labor was implemented when Roman civilization was in decline.

Intelligence gradually ceased to be a universal characteristic of humanity at the end of medieval civilization, at the time of the weakening of the huge communitarian edifice built by the joint efforts of social groups and the

---

1   *Virtus domitiva*, "dormitive power," is a term coined by Molière in his play *Le Malade imaginaire* (1673), a satire on hypochondria and quacks in the medical profession, to explain why opium causes sleep. When a medical student is asked why opium induces sleep he responds that it is because it has dormitive power. This phrase has come to denote a vacuous explanation.

Church. And now in a similar period when organic social structures weaken and fissures develop in relations among people, the burgeoning of modern specialization becomes more extensive. Examples of this abound. Let us cite some specific cases. It is significant that the family doctor – who formed bonds bordering on the affective with those close to the patient, intimately united to the family, providing moral support – is increasingly replaced by the specialist enclosed in his clinic, who only grants a limited amount of time to the patient. Also, it is remarkable that the philosopher – who by vocation should experience a relationship with the universe, and the totality of being, to raise it to the level of his thought – is in our day transformed into a man as specialized and as distant as possible from all dynamic contact with nature, that is, into the professor. Finally, it is striking that the politician – whose function should be to consolidate or maintain social bonds – has become under the guise of a journalist, press agent, or member of parliament, an artisan specializing in the rupture of these ties; it is striking that he is not part of social groups unless they can be disrupted by sophistic propaganda and election campaigning.

DIVISION OF LABOR

The phenomenon which is the key to the transformations of our age is the breakup of organic social structures (family, trade or profession, region, town (the true homeland), where people had previously been gathered together into a close community to which they belonged from birth), which we have witnessed as though blind, or winking as we snicker, at times with unctuousness, for the past one or two centuries.

It explains to us right from the start the form which the division of labor currently takes. In the broad sense of the word, this has always existed, like the technical itself. One would have difficulty in identifying a single period of history when it was absent. The distribution of chores in families living the traditional lives of farmers or craftsmen is a clear example of this. The father, who is in charge, brings the tasks of working the earth or plying his craft to completion, with his steady, skilled hands. The mother manages the home and supplies the family's needs. The children help out here and there with their little jobs. The servants, if there are any, assist in the preliminary, most basic tasks and with the heavy work. The old fable of the limbs and the stomach symbolizes this approach, which today we term primitive.[2] It also brings out the essential characteristic of the division of labor in the milieu of natural communities: just as in a healthy, well-developed body the actions, internal or external, of all organs work together and mutually support each other, the diversity of functions is the product of the dynamic unity of the social group and always works to strengthen it. A philosopher would say that the division of labor is inherent in a natural social group and always oriented towards it. In other words, the social regulates the economic, which is dependent on it, just as the soul fills the various organs of the living body and constrains them to form a unity. There is, however, a form of the division of labor that abstracts itself from the social group and then comes back to place itself above the organic unity of the group.

In devitalized societies, the division of labor exists, but a basic difference, unperceived, makes it adopt a different plan: no longer ordered by the social body, it becomes autonomous. The characteristics of the technological approach and contemporary economics derive from this absurd situation.

PRODUCTION FOR THE SAKE OF PRODUCTION

In the first place, work no longer has as its objective – formerly present unconsciously – to give the social group

---

2 The fable goes back to ancient times. The moral of the fable is that teamwork is essential.

a firmer cohesion, indispensable to it. It no longer brings with it economic activity which gives sustenance, materially and spiritually, in the way that nourishment sustains the body, and thus the soul. Work and its specialization will from now on have only one possible objective, production, continual production, and nothing more. Work becomes an activity directed only towards the product, *disengaged from the worker*, resulting in his alienation. This situation cannot be remedied by arteriosclerotic social channels. The *homo naturaliter politicus*[3] is transformed into *homo oeconomicus*, with all the consequences ruthlessly set in motion by Marx.

From this point of view, we can say that if Marx's intuition was brilliant, it was too short-sighted and terribly compromised at its first clash.[4] Marx in no way saw that the economic is normally an integral part of the social, which tempers and refines it, thus elevating and vitalizing it. As a result, it launches contemporary man onto a dead-end path as it attempts to put an end to the alienation of man through the myth of a pseudo-social-technical-economic approach which only infinitely increases this alienation. Far from curing man, communism perpetuates his illness. He is doomed due to a lie which eternally postpones to the future the social truth which it cannot attain and towards which alienated man rushes with his vague aspirations.

The obsession with the economic which haunts us has no other origin than our blindness to the compelling necessity of restoring our natural social structures, thus eliminating the numerous middlemen between producer and consumer, a situation which increasingly requires – what a farce! – an economy which betrays its role. To produce in order to live, to live in order to produce, such is the vicious circle where the beginning and the end automatically refer back

3   Latin, man is political by nature.
4   De Corte may be referring to the Russian revolution in 1917.

to each other, in a huge cycle, encompassing under its arcs an increased number of middlemen since it has no other way to get bigger! In fact, modern man can do nothing but produce: it is impossible for him to live, except in the most physical meaning of the word, since the limitation of the technical to production and life indwelling in man mutually repel each other, as long as the individual who works and makes an effort to live is not included within the organic communities which could reconcile them. The principle of the homo oeconomicus thus becomes: produce for the sake of producing, an endless recurring nightmare which causes a paralyzing neurotic frenzy. Jung's axiom in all its breadth applies here: neurosis is caused by a life not lived, by a life whose substance flows out of it and congeals like a clot of blood. In an incredible paradox, production then amounts to destruction, impoverishment, and crisis.

THE ROBOTIC MAN

On the other hand, specialization and technology, left to themselves, without being counterbalanced by their integration into a social sphere vitalized by organic relationships, inevitably lead to the atomization of man and his absorption into the routine of his work. Man isolated from his social context becomes in some way diminished through his work, which takes on a mechanical character to the degree that it is deprived of that warmth and dynamism inherent in social life. Then there arises a complication about the cause of this which gives us the key to a phenomenon which sociologists have never stopped arguing about: is it the development of man which brings about the great proliferation of all sorts of technologies which are suffocating us now, or on the contrary is it the evolution of techniques which modify human behavior, to the point of making it unrecognizable? In reality, there is no other alternative, and the two competing theses are correct. The words "development" and "evolution" employed here are as erroneous as possible regarding the linear image they conjure up: they mask the real process, which is cyclical. The collapse of traditional social structures is in fact accompanied by stages which follow each other according to a relentless deterministic process, returning to the point of departure in order to go through the cycle again with increasing virulence: solitude corresponding to man's state in the world; the impossibility for him to communicate other than through his work, now devitalized and mechanized; the extension of this automatism in the invention of new techniques which supply for human deficiencies; mechanization; increasing solitude experienced by man incapable of finding a new viable way to become integrated into a new technological world; pressure resulting from the growing mechanical character of society, an effect of technology, affecting traditional social structures, now eroded; the increasing danger of the collapse of these structures. Then the cycle begins again: the response of man to adapt to the world of technology by the only means at his disposal, to learn about technology; modification of traditional modes of behavior due to the influence of technical approaches to both industry and society, where these methodologies now work in consort; the tendency towards the ultimate technicalization of man, the world, and society; the manifestation of a belief in the "new man" who communicates to others a sense of forgetfulness, if not of scorn, of the past. And so the circular movement begins yet again, in theory continuing indefinitely, until the appearance of the "robotic man."

In the immense loss of the living communion of people with each other we see a deficit which no communitarian, personalist system, socialist or communist, will ever manage to compensate for, though they were invented to make up for this lack.

The human being immersed in an atmosphere rich with social exchanges in some way opens up all the possibilities of his own being as he participates in the social body, which is like an extension of his own being: an invisible body, intangible, self-evident, whose presence is felt by man in his lived everyday experience, the elements of which he perceives intuitively: relatives, neighbors, friends, work associates, landscapes . . . Nothing can match the plenitude of the expansive feeling, once our daily labor has come to an end, which comes over us around the common table, in a fraternal ambience, on a park bench, chatting with people from the area whom we encounter, or while we are alone and lost in thought. With each job-related task, the work man has undertaken assumes a meaning which goes beyond him, mysterious, inaccessible to consciousness due to its complexity, which is awkwardly expressed by the word "communion": work has entered into the living circuitry of the community, as the worker experiences the support of a vast body which expands his soul. Isolated by his individual task, he stretches out at the end of the work day, with the secret joy of being more than he seems to be, without being aware of it. And every day is a witness to this systolic and diastolic process.

But a person who has nothing but his work loses himself in his job, or, more often, for he must pretend to have an intrinsic vitality that is no longer his, in the economic benefit which seems to mimic this vitality and which makes a return to him. His whole being is invested in the things which he makes or in money, that is to say, in objects. Now objects do not communicate among themselves: the power of communion is radically lacking to them. They exist side by side, external to each other in the space which they share. Under the spell of the prestige of technological civilization, implemented by the mechanism of the division of labor, man is side by side with other men, his brothers, without communicating with them, like one object among others. He is no longer defined by his organic relationship to a group, but by his place next to others, like a gear engaging with another gear. The expressions to have a job, to find, lose, or look for employment, show us how far man considers himself an object. In the world of technology, moreover, no one is irreplaceable and each person can be moved about with a minimum of harm.

Collectivism, then, arises under the sway of material causes as powerful as those which control molecules and which can be reduced to several fundamental laws.

THE TWO ASPECTS OF COLLECTIVISM

In the first place, man in the grip of technology is inevitably demeaned: the fact that a technical civilization is clearly a civilization of the masses confirms this. Man descends like a dead weight and his energy is debased to the level of the most limiting material determinism possible. No longer self-directing but objectified, having become a thing, he is subject to the laws governing things. But every fall from a previously well-structured whole produces rubble which forms a mass. The consequences are the geographical agglomeration of towns, concentrations of political power, coarseness of physical appearance, and a debased aesthetics: it is enough to take a look at the lumpenproletariat of our suburbs.[5] Yet these are only the superficial manifestations of the phenomenon of collectivism, which leads to the primacy of technology.

The increasing division of labor, unchecked, without a doubt ends up with specialization at the upper ranks, as is quite apparent, but it equally leads to specialization at the lower levels of society, too often ignored. When in a milieu energized by a network of organic social exchanges, this division brings with it the complementarity of the lower and upper echelons, the convergence of efforts whether manual or intellectual, the necessary intervention of thought, opinion, and physical strength

---

5   In some European cities the suburbs are generally the equivalent of our inner cities.

of all parties, in different degrees as determined by the perceptions and experience of all. On the contrary, in a mechanized sphere of activity, cut off from living social relationships, the division of labor separates people into two distinct groups: manual workers and intellectual workers, those whose thoughts and persons are directed to things and their production, and those whom James Burnham calls the managers.[6] This dividing line is as visible in the socialist as in the capitalist regime. Why is this? Because technology disassociated from the social fabric requires it.

Unfettered technology has as its end increased production. This obviously assumes a greater cooperation among those who combine their efforts into one unique effort. This cooperation unites fragmented activities into a single collective action and gathers workers together to form a kind of giant worker: factory, firm, store . . . The language of advertising is revealing: it refers to the products of one or another corporate group.

This must then be said and said again: an artificial bond which combines several movements into one will never be effected without the intervention of one and only one mind. It is futile to believe that a collective mind accompanies the birth of the collectivity. A collective mind does not and cannot exist. The number "2" in Paul's mind and the number "2" in Pierre's mind will never be added together to make the number "4" in the "collective mind" shared by Pierre and Paul. Only the mind of Paul or the mind of Peter is capable of making this connection. Similarly, the idea of each worker about his segment of work can be ordered to someone else's idea only from within one and the same mind which is intractably external to both of them. A collective "mind" is completely incapable of thinking: its existence is only a matter of words or the

---

6   James Burnham, 1905-1987, American who wrote on political theory. In his important work, *The Managerial Revolution*, he envisioned the possibility of managers engaged in a struggle for social control as the ruling class.

imagination. Consequently, as Simone Weil says, "in order that the efforts of several may be united, they must all be directed by one and the same mind."[7] This is the meaning of the well-known verse from Faust "one mind is enough for a thousand hands." The regimes where the primacy of technology was established all evolved, to different degrees, in a monarchical or, even better, dictatorial direction: Stalin, Roosevelt and his New Deal, Truman and his Marshall Plan, Attlee and his nationalizations are witnesses to this, more or less forthright, more or less attenuated by antagonistic forces.[8]

This is precisely because there is no collective mind, because collectivity exists as a mass devoid of thought, affectivity, or the capacity for communion and social relations. The drama of "the woman without a head" of whom Maurras speaks when referring to democracy can also be attributed to the economy.[9] Such is the type of man who develops contemporary technology to its limit. Let no one be mistaken about this. Everyone is immersed in its seductive sphere of influence, since if technologies working in parallel usher us into the "age of managers",

---

7   Simone Weil, 1909-1943, French philosopher, political activist, and admirer of Catholicism, which she never formally embraced. Initially attracted to Marxism, she later criticized communism, fascism, and exploitative capitalism. The quotation is from "Réflexions sur les causes de la liberté et de l'oppression sociale" (1934) in *Oppression et liberté* (1955). From the cited paragraph of Weil's essay De Corte borrows her example of the impossibility of adding together numbers in the minds of two individuals, and also repeats her quote from Faust.

8   The Marshall plan, proposed by Secretary of State George Marshall in 1947 and enacted the following year, provided aid to Western Europe. Over thirteen billion dollars was transferred, with the largest sums going to the major industrial powers. Clement Richard Attlee, 1883-1967, Labour Party leader and prime minister of Great Britain 1945-1951. Attlee nationalized about twenty percent of the British economy, including railroads, electricity, the coal and steel industries, and the Bank of England. One is surprised to see De Corte categorize Stalin with figures such as Roosevelt, Truman, and Atlee. Perhaps this is due to his vehement opposition to centralization.

9   Charles Maurras, 1868-1952, French politician, social critic, and poet, and a major force behind Action Française, a royalist, anti-parliamentary and pro-Catholic movement. The "woman without a head" refers to the Third French Republic.

the turbulent masses will not fail to take hold of them in turn. The critique of capitalism which makes a distinction between the oppressed and the oppressors and the critique of communism which contrasts slaves with the Master give way to a more profound critique which assimilates the victim to the executioner and the executioner to the victim. It is clear that the management of the masses requires the manager to put himself at their level: a physical object can only be moved by physical energy. It is a truth of the first order that a residual belief in a transcendent God runs the risk of making us forget: The robotic man will be directed by a robotic man, the machine by a machine. The manager himself is engulfed in the mechanics of his organization. The more men submit to the requirements for collaboration demanded by technology, the more will they be dealt with as objects by the ideology which brings them together, but even more will this ideology necessarily act on them by the only means which destabilizes things: physical power. It is superfluous to emphasize the appalling mechanical thought of so many businessmen. All ideas about implementing technology which are not counter-balanced by the prior presence of organic communities become tyrannical, that is to say, as Plato demonstrates, they are oriented towards servility, since they depend on the slavery which they institute and on the human material which they utilize.[10] The master is a slave just like the slave, the oppressor is oppressed like the one oppressed, and thought is material just like matter. Though it may be disassociated for a short while from the collectivity which it controls, the dominant ideology always returns to it when it takes action. Collectivism and universal materialism, characteristic of the technological civilization, thus have a common root: they need each other, and the collective man is nothing other than man become matter-bound

---

10   See his *Republic* for commentary of slavery, e.g., the one under tyranny is a slave "in the highest possible degree" (577c).

energy, as much in his soul as in his body, subjected, like matter, to the law of entropy.

This is why a civilization where the technical reigns follows a second line of action which is increasingly manifested before our eyes. Devoid of the organic relations which run through the fabric of the natural communities to which people are destined, it must create out of nothing new social bonds which emphasize its inherent collectivism. A purely technical society is really a monster, since technology is incapable, on its own, of being social. It simply finds places for all persons, putting them side by side, meshing them together. The merely external union which it imposes and the combination of individual efforts which it brings together into one sole enterprise do not originate in the minds or hearts of the people it gathers together. Thus the civilization is unstable, restless, agitated. In order to last, it must establish a new social order, capable of maintaining the unity of its components.

It will be a matter of building a new community whose members fuse together, according to the technical plan, into one sole gigantic individual. The operation is accomplished by means of the only door which remains open within the devitalized, dispirited people: the imagination, where base mythologies rush in. A technical "society" stays in place only through the myths it creates about itself, embedding itself in them. These may differ from one country to the next, but they are expressed in just one model: the establishment of the social group into a bloc where every sector is attracted to just one "idea" which transcends all of them, and situates them, through the intermediary of institutional or semi-institutional structures, within the gravitational field of the economy. This is the "great beast" referred to by Plato in his *Republic*, which today catches the imagination of the people, even if not seen in actual events, through the universal attraction of its inherent dynamism.

From this perspective, the superficial differences between capitalism and communism diminish to the point of disappearing. Where technology reigns absolutely, new institutions arise which can only be socialist. Marx sees better than anyone that the economic infrastructure orders the superstructure of the state, but, here as everywhere in his work, his barren intuition misses the mark, since this situation only obtains in the case of societies where technology penetrates to the core and where statism must embrace the dictum that one mind suffices for a thousand hands and then proceed apace. This, we believe, is the only possible conception of the multifaceted socialism which is found everywhere in contemporary "society."

An exclusively technical civilization which repudiates natural communities can only cope with the social disorder which it provokes by means of an extension of its centralizing strategy: in clashes among the *membra disjecta*[11] of its internal economy, it responds by nationalizations, and in conflicts among peoples, by internationalization. It must give rise to a *homo politicus* analogous to the *homo oeconomicus*, whose spontaneous social reactions coalesce to form the unique power of the state. Through universal suffrage, military service, government benefits, and yet a thousand other additional measures, our contemporaries increasingly merge into a single mass which the political state – in fact, the economic state – manipulates as it wishes, without their having the least organic relationship among themselves. Today we are in all likelihood in the last stage of this process.

Under the increasingly transparent veil of a democracy – liberal or popular – two analogous forms of the same technological ideology, which are only antagonistic in the measure to which they have not yet been realized on a worldwide scale, give birth to the collective man. Whichever form comes into being, the result will be identical: the universal "great beast" rises up at the end of the adventure.

---

11   Latin, scattered fragments or members.

THE GREAT BEAST

The "great beast" is taking on an undeniably economic character. We see it take shape, become undone, and recreate itself before our eyes, in all countries, under the form of cartels, trusts, and nationalizations, with its pecuniary tentacles, like a specter looking for its body and bringing with it the maelstrom of the transmigration of souls. Pacts among its various elements are made and unmade. Sometimes it is established, by ruse or violence, only to come to an end shortly afterwards in the course of wars and revolutions. Unstable in its essence, like matter, ready to assume all forms, again like matter, internally rent apart by its components who are mutually sealed off from each other and by the individuals without humane social bonds who form it, pulled in opposite directions by its managers who fight among themselves for control, it is doomed to be born in order to die, and to be reborn in perpetuity. This polymorphism, these rises and falls, can be explained: the "great beast" of production always tends to grow and become global, because of the way it works, since increased division of labor requires closer collaboration, yet it always tends to disintegrate, collapse, and pick itself back up in limited geographical areas, inasmuch as it is only a "great beast" of finance, incapable of forming the least viable relationships among people. When it grows beyond a certain size, the purely material links which it maps out among its different components become so complex and entangled that they destabilize. In order to maintain its own equilibrium, each component separates itself from the whole, which compromises it, threatening its own existence. On the other hand, the needs which the "great beast" of economics has created are determinative for its new distended growth. They want to be filled to excess, requiring a worldwide system, yet as their point of origin and the division of labor involve particular specifications, they introduce into the global system of management an unassimilable complexity which provokes its demise.

Our contemporaries do not perceive that the "great beast" is incapable of assuming a true body because it is incapable of possessing a soul, and that it is incapable of possessing a soul because by its very nature it lacks basic organic relationships. The truth is that the collective man generated by modern technology *does not exist*; he is always in the process of becoming, ceaselessly seeking an overarching conceptual structure that will enable him to exist. This is what Marxists call dialectic: thesis, antithesis, synthesis, and then the process begins again. The "great beast" exists only in the imagination of people today. This accounts for its enormous prestige. No one is unaware that it has become, for millions, the object of an exclusive cult: the history of the last two centuries is replete with upheavals which give rise to this specter. Starting with the phase when economics comes to the fore, it penetrates politics, morals, customs, even surmounting the ramparts erected by its opponents. It encircles itself with a halo of piety: the bloody sacrifices it demands are no longer the product of the imagination, but are found in what happens in everyday life. The "great beast" represents for moderns what the fetish is for primitive people. It is the *idol* par excellence.

THE BIRTH OF THE "GREAT BEAST"

Why have technology and the masses been transformed into idols? There is only one answer: the "great beast" is the projection, the magnification, of innumerable real "little beasts." As it is only one idol, it is the grossly enlarged image of the self, the "me," the inflated "me," the hollow "me." As long as viable social bonds among people persist, idolatry is not possible: the organic nature of the social body itself hinders the magnification of the self. In the great days of the ancient state, pagan religion was not idolatrous in the full sense of the word. St. Paul's address at the Areopagus gives evidence of this. "Athenians, I see that in every respect you are eminently religious!" [Acts 17:22]. No more than the barbarians did the Greeks and Romans adore totally false gods: they anthropomorphized God; they did not exaggerate the human being. Nothing horrified them more than hubris. Their epics and tragedies are full of this fear. They maintained respect for the transcendent. For the base, divinized countenance of the "great beast" to appear on earth, there first had to come the fall of the empire, social disorder resulting from its collapse, and the rupture of all human ties to the profit of a huge bureaucratic machinery. In fact, the ancient "great beast" can be completely distinguished from ours: it was only actualized in a restricted number of individuals, as the others passively abandoned themselves to their fate. Very few aspired to it due to a lack of adequate technical means. The *homo oeconomicus* had not yet been born, free of every real social relationship, having only his own *image* before him, no longer with any limitations in his efforts to project it onto the world except for one: money. What is the only obstacle, save that one, keeping man from enjoying the benefits of widespread technology?

The imaginary "great beast," set up as an idol, came forth out of the will to obliterate this obstacle. In former times, the isolated individual, separated from his natural communities, inevitably met with failure. If he was not equipped with a strong soul and determined will, he was crushed by solitude, shriveled up within a mediocre life. Possessed of money, he is found everywhere today, unscathed. Technology offers him an infinitude of ways to avoid failure. As for the others, the destitute, the excluded, the dispossessed, they have already been co-opted by the very mechanism of technology: side by side, they form part of the masses, and they are aware of this, for the interruption of every organic rhythm of life immediately brings this to consciousness. Caught in the huge pseudo-social machinery which technology has set up, in their collective action itself they run up against an obstacle identical to the one they surmount every day: money, which is an object like the objects they manufacture. Only a small obscure residue from their heritage, political or religious, can slow down their progress. Why could they not dream of a victory similar to one they have? They imagine that one huge revolutionary effort, the fruit of many individuals working together as one, would create a hypertechnical "society" from which could be eliminated the last barrier separating them from themselves, from their "I" which wishes to blossom, held in check by only one thing. They cannot do other than adore the imagined disappearance of the unfinished collective entity which they constitute and whose ill-defined possibilities they experience every day, because the idol of the collective promises them salvation. It would be easy to show here that capitalist and communist modes of operation are completely identical, with the same "humane" methods, the former taking the top-down approach and the latter the bottom-up approach, the same "I" asserting itself, the same grandiose "little beast." All the rest, individuality, personality, dignity of man, justice, liberty, etc. is nothing but literary production, mediocre at that, empty philosophy and sociology where the "I" gropingly examines itself, finds and adores itself.

Abstract concepts, cast in universal terms, do not have the same content, which depends on whether they flourish in a healthy social climate where life has sown them, or whether they bear fruit in an unhealthy social climate where a rootless imagination has scattered them about. This is like sugar in the body of a man in good health or in a diabetic. What is nourishment for the soul is transformed into poison when the societal organ which produces it removes itself from the laws governing the body or when the body degenerates.

THE COLLECTIVE UNITY

The most subtle of poisonous alkaloids is undoubtedly the idea of unity propagated by modern technology in the minds of our contemporaries, penetrating even to their unconscious reflex reactions. They tunefully proclaim to us, in all keys, that the unity of the world and of people is in the process of being achieved thanks to technology: Do we not have need of each other more than ever in order to live? Yet, looking at it closely, we see that this unity is only imaginary. It could only exist in one mind capable of coordinating the various actions required for production into one unique action. As this mind does not exist, except in embryonic form, it must be created in the imagination. Even supposing that it could come into being, it would be necessary for the masses which it automatically brings into existence to be capable of thinking, or, failing that, of living. But the masses neither think nor live. They are a passive entity and have at their disposal only the imagination, like a slave who can only dream of his freedom. It is thus necessary to develop the imagination of the masses to the maximum. All the candidates for the position of the theoretician behind planetary unity are used to this. What can the masses dream of being except that they should be everything, since they are nothing? Without any internal unity, the masses are all the more inclined to imagine it, to hold onto it, since they will always be deprived of it inasmuch as they are the masses, like the condemned person whose fate depends on obtaining pardon from a malevolent prince continually dreams of what is impossible for him to believe. This supposition invades his whole being, becomes merged with his very self; the pardon can only come from within himself, since there is no other path to it. The masses can only believe in obtaining favor from themselves. The technological regime denies any other possibility for them: "Proletarians of all countries, unite!"[12] In other words, the masses believe in the masses as in a divine savior: they are walled up within their own divinity. The masses are the opium of the working class.

Coming from the pseudo-social approach imposed on people by technology, the idol of collective unity is contradictory. On the one hand, the idol can only begin to achieve this unity by means of the very technology which has brought it into being. How could it actually create itself without technical methods, the only ones at its disposal, since it despises, rejects, or is unaware of the traditional tools for life in common? On the other hand, the idol cannot have recourse to technical methods without exacerbating the fate of the masses spawned by them. This is why the idol of unity becomes more distant to the degree that it is near, seeming to be within reach. The closer we are to its countenance, the more it reveals itself in its consuming horror. It has to die in order to be born. Its truth begins with lies.

As bitter as this affirmation may be to our pride, technology cannot give us anything which is socially viable. It reveals a collectivity of human beings lacking organic relationships who form a mass and who build a civilization whose charge, the most remarkable one we have heard of, is to call unity and freedom what people always commonly called chaos and slavery. In this sense, it is important to eliminate with utmost rigor an idea that today no longer has any currency, the concept of class. The collectivity which develops under the influence of technology does not entail any class structure: all people who form part of the collectivity, masters and slaves, are oppressed, since they are all subjected to the influence of the exclusively material spirit of technology. To claim with Marxists that capitalism frees a few members of the privileged class, possessing the means of production, and enslaves all the rest, is an absurd statement which does not stand up to scrutiny. There is no oppressor class; there is only an oppressive structure

---

12   A rallying slogan from Marx's *Communist Manifesto* (1848).

belonging to the pseudo-society and arising from a technology not providing the framework for any living community.

It is moreover important to oppose the idiotic slogan in widespread use even in Christian milieus, the liberation of man through technology. It certainly cannot be denied that in many areas technology has freed man from the power of nature. Yet this liberation brings with it terrible consequences: the enslavement of man to the collectivity. It is possible to escape from the forces of nature simply by moving to another place. It is all the more impossible to escape from the collective as on the one hand it provides one's daily bread, while on the other hand, as all its effects are imaginary, it encloses man within the unassailable fortress of himself.

The inexorable task of the collective is to imprison the human being within himself, sealing off all openings by which he could be connected to what is outside himself.

THE SELF AND THE COLLECTIVE

The psycho-sociological process is of such importance that it requires careful examination. Collectivity, in the proper meaning of the word, exists, as we have said, only on the economic level of intensified production where each element of the whole is necessarily considered as part of a single synchronized effort. Yet the pressures brought to bear by the economy and the decline of organic social groups are so pronounced that contemporary man can only understand himself as forming an integral part of a whole and, at the same time, as an isolated self. He is at once alone in a social desert and in solidarity with the material destiny of humanity. This contradictory situation defines the essence of modern man, cut off from his own mind by technology and from social groups due to his devitalization, empty on the one hand, inflated on the other, reduced to his elastic surface like a balloon. In fact, emptiness and pomposity complement each other and make up his *pretentiousness*. The clearest outcome of the development of a technological civilization and of the anemic condition of natural societies is the proliferation of pretentious individuals who believe that they are everything when they are nothing. The hubris which seems to affect our age is, in the last analysis, reduced to lilliputian dimensions. Indeed, the specialized competence which is exercised in a limited zone of one's being without encountering any obstacles intensifies the feeling of a self living outside a social framework.

His area of expertise gives man the conviction that he could dominate what is universal from the height of his littleness. The two factors of technicism and the devaluation of natural communities join their efforts with one and the same aim: the transcendence of the self. However, each individual self experiences a connection to other similar selves within the powerful machinery that exploits the world's riches, resulting in even greater ambition for the self as it achieves a kind of cosmic regency. Each individual consciousness thus feels itself to be a universal consciousness. But a universal consciousness does not, and cannot, exist; such an expression is only empty chatter. There is merely a dust cloud of selves, led by the momentum of technological civilization engulfing them, moving each to consider himself as the master of the world.

In this deleterious climate, every man outrageously claims to be everyman, bearing within himself the destiny of humanity. Since many find themselves in an identical situation, they all imagine that they communicate with each other from within a worldwide collectivity, when they are prisoners of a common illusion which prevents them from forming the least viable relationship with each other. There are numerous examples of each self sequestered within itself in the same way, enclosed within the same fiction as within a protective armor that confirms it in its unassailable presumption that it is everything. This is why the failure or anxiety of another self has repercussions from one end to the other of the mass formed by identical atoms, like an impact sustained by one end of an iron rod is felt by all the molecules in it. An event is felt as a personal injury or victory without the least rudimentary organic relationship to serve as basis for this reaction: the fact that everyone is in the same situation is enough to provoke a reaction in each self, walled up inside itself, without leading to the least actual social exchange, without anyone having to go out of himself and his absolute solitude. The metaphor of the iron rod could be replaced here by one of empty space into which objects of various weights falling from a height descend at the same speed. Collective man, whose thoughts are communicated via so many intellectuals, is like empty space into which individuals fall, whatever their level or their intelligence, or their dialectic ineptness or facility. Clothed with the same inorganic existence, with a merely verbal connection with each other, they all commune from within nothingness. It is superfluous to add that nothing shuts up a man within himself more effectively than communal participation in non-being: in the absence of life, there is no movement of life.

We must say it again: collective man is an individual who imagines himself identified with humanity because he is constrained to do so by economic collectivism, associated with the organic decline of the social body. Collectivism is individualism taken to the limit and materially subjected to the law of human gravity. This modest and striking truth is slowly becoming known. The facts show it, advance it, and impose it. If the mind still refuses to accept what they teach, the very flesh of man receives their painful stamp, which awakens the most stubborn from their dogmatic slumber. This rule admits of no exceptions, even when there seems to be one, since the clever who escape from this "ultimate anthill" enter through the low doorway of political parties or ideologies which determine even more absolutely their lot: every heresy receives disciplinary action, as it must, under the penalty of having the fiction immediately explode into rubble.

THE MYSTIFICATION OF COLLECTIVISM

The collectivist mystique is the driving force and the goal of the pseudo-society where technology alone reigns. Yet it is also the most incredible deception in history, defended by an army of academics, intellectuals, and "spiritual" persons, all without roots moreover, and subject to the mystification of the "collective man," the imaginary, pitiful reflection of the conditions of production in the souls of our contemporaries. The famous arguments of Marx (and of Feuerbach) against religion backfire here. [13] We know that according to orthodox atheism, God is only a fantasy, the product of a delusion through which man tries to escape from the condition imposed on him by capitalism.

We do not completely deny the appositeness of this analysis: it is only too clear that man has a singular propensity to divinize his own image. However, he does not resort only to idolatry to flee from his fate or anesthetize his sorrow. Even more frequently, he makes an idol of himself to confirm his good conscience with regard to himself. We can have no doubt, for example, that the good of bourgeois deism is the divinized projection of a universal order which leads in the end to the "laissez-faire" of each individual: everything "works out" in the abstract as it does in the imagination. It is the same with the idea of the collective man, a degradation of deism, transcendent when viewed from the level of a dull, mediocre humanity. This serves as a justification for the materialism of our contemporaries. For no dialectical ramblings can obscure this fundamental fact: the sole

---

13 Marx, *Critique of Hegel's Philosophy of Right*, 1843: "Religion is the sigh of the oppressed creature, the heart of a heartless world, and the soul of a soulless condition. It is the opium of the people." Ludwig Feuerbach, 1804–1872, German philosopher and anthropologist. In his *The Essence of Christianity*, 1841, he holds that God is a projection of man, a chimera.

raison d'être for a humanity which sees the source of its organic social relations dry up and which witnesses the limitless development of its industrial strength can only be the exploitation of matter, since it is constrained to look for a substitute for its depleted reserves of live-giving energy.

Yet no man or no system would dare to admit this deficiency. The most daring of them boast about their "scientific" materialism, immediately adding: for the greatest good of the collectivity. Others, with more cunning, take the "spiritualistic" approach: what fortunate opportunities technology offers for the development of the "spirit," unburdened of its most thankless tasks! Everyone forecasts a new golden age for humanity, under the guise of a collectivity which does not exist. The collective is the imaginary idol which absolves their bad consciences and restores them to their original goodness; it is the god which fictitiously gathers together scattered individual selves in their greed as it now draws all earthly goods to itself as its exclusive possession. In handing himself over to the imaginary collectivity, each individual entrusts himself to himself with complete peace of mind. In making a sacrifice of himself, each puts himself on a pedestal. Holding "the human consciousness as the highest divinity," in the words of Marx, each man sets himself up as a little despotic god of a huge "hornet's nest."[14]

The collective only exacerbates this situation in its two variants: the "batrachomyomachia"[15] and the reign of the *homo loquax*[16] where personalities are weak, and the "titanomachia"[17] and the triumph of the strongest, where

---

14 From Marx, *The Difference between the Democritean and Epicurean Philosophy of Nature*, doctoral dissertation, 1841.
   "Hornet's nest," *panier de crabes* in French, literally "basket of crabs." This expression refers to a group of people who could be working together, but instead are at each other's throats.
15 *Batrachomyomachia*, *The Battle of the Frogs and Mice*, parody of the *Iliad*, sometimes attributed to Homer.
16 Latin, chattering man, or chatterbox.
17 *War of the Titans*, poem of ancient Greece, author unknown. Titans were sometimes seen as being in between gods and men.

the personalities are without scruples: the talkative self who aims to convert others and ensnares them over with words in order to dominate them, as opposed to the violent self who enslaves them through fear. We add here the cruel expression of Clemenceau, "one can always hold two positions at the same time."[18]

We can never overemphasize the fact that the collectivist critique of "bourgeois" individualism is in reality a confession made in bad faith which projects onto others its own misdeeds. For devotion to the collective, which has only an imaginary existence, that is, within the self, is nothing but devotion to oneself and to one's own excellence. This solicitude, conveyed via soulless bureaucratic methods, multiplies to infinity the egotistical betrayal effected by the "bourgeois."

Here again the technological model which imposes itself on contemporary "society" wreaks havoc. The goal is to collaborate in a mechanical fashion so that all may attain to "happiness" without experiencing organic relationships, now regarded as superfluous, and, for that matter, too demanding. The expected outcome will never resemble what mass production with its technology yields: no matter what efforts are made, man is not a manufactured object. To benefit from collective mechanization, man then has only one course of action: to pretend to be an object, to mesh his activity as skillfully as possible with the cogwheels of the machine, to imitate its anonymous nature, to adapt his existence to its imaginary existence, in other words to imagine having what he does not have or being what he is not, or even to commit "fraud." This is what produces government benefits, for instance. It is moreover

---

18   Georges Clemenceau, 1841-1929, French statesman who successfully led France during the post-World War I period. He was possibly referring to the fact that he himself held two different positions, Prime Minister and Minister of War, 1917-1920. He had previously been both Prime Minister and Minister of the Interior, 1906-1909. Or the remark may have had a more cynical context.

a known fact that in this area, the collectivist interventions are all the less common when vital, that is to say strictly humane, concerns come into play. The imaginary and the real are antagonistic to each other. The only tangible result from collectivist interventions of this type is the technical apparatus, sufficient unto itself, which combines together the various egotistical interests found in different quarters.

UNDER THE SIGN OF THE ABSTRACT

Thus we find a great contradiction between the abstract and concrete running through every civilization in decline. As prodigious as the technology of our civilization may be, and as extensive the collective automation which it spawns may be, taken as a whole they are something delusory. In both cases, man becomes quite incapable of experiencing the relationship between his work and its result: the abstract stamp of the overall technological program or the administrative machinery with its red tape intervenes, like an insurmountable wall, between them, blocking and repressing the flow of what energy he has left, now fated to dissipate under the dark shadow cast by the sign of the abstract. We should consider here the effort of the person under the yoke of the division of labor, of the monotony of work devoid of interest, of political and social interventions which get lost within a whole which is quite impossible to grasp: his soul, his life, and his mind have no concrete objective which is comprehended, lived, humanized, within an organic vision of the whole. Everything contributes to the substitution of the abstract, what is schematic and unreal, constitutive of technological thinking and its social superstructure, for his life and thought. Now the characteristic of the sign of the abstract, left to itself, is to multiply like bad seed. The less man lives and thinks within concrete reality as a whole, the more new, supplementary abstract signs are required, and the thicker the wall separating his efforts from their outcome. The sign proliferates at the expense of what is signified, to the detriment of men, the distinctions among whom are erased in the wake of abstractions. In order to be understood by the initiated, their brood requires what Simone Weil calls "signs for signs,"[19] culminating in the only supreme sign there can be on earth, the national state, soon to be worldwide, governed by a few in the name of universal Democracy, and which, having been neither experienced nor conceived by them, assimilates them as if it were "the perfect and ultimate anthill."[20]

We believe that it is impossible, in the present circumstances, to slow down the movement towards centralization based on abstractions. Beginning with the political, continuing with the technical, then implemented on the social level, it advances like an overpowering tidal wave. Modern man, devitalized, bereft of the spiritual, gives himself over to the automatism of the abstract imagination, the only faculty which consoles him in his uprooted condition, acting on him like a secular religion that is debased and stupefying. The abstract imagination is indeed the locus of all possibilities, including the impossible, and as a result reality, which is patient, still, and eternal, shatters it, reducing it to nothingness. Between that which is and which lasts, and that which cannot be and will never come into being, it makes for itself a straight path, and as though sleepwalking, proceeds through its stages, one after the other, with a marvelous dexterity just like an unconscious surveyor. Thanks to the technical aspects of the political "organization," today everything is possible, no matter what the obstacle. Nothing can stop this succession of events, except a catastrophe, since what is an impossibility today will become a possibility tomorrow: it is enough to demolish concrete reality as it asserts itself in the deceptive imagination, putting up all the less resistance

19   *La pesenteur et la grâce*, 1947.
20   Paul Valéry, *La Crise de l'esprit*, 1919.

the more its internal organic bonds are undermined in numerous spheres. People today are powerfully assisted in their labors by their dread of the suffering which liberating technology seems capable of eliminating as it releases them from the burden of the laws of nature, which always entail an admixture of joy and bitterness. Incapable of forming natural social bonds among themselves, they are for this reason incapable of comprehending the constant connection between evil and good in earthly existence. This is why they are blind to the evil they do and the suffering they cause. They dream of an unalloyed good, imaginary, devoid of the least hint of evil. Technology, which affects all areas of life, subjugating nature, seems to them to be the way to achieve it. In order to get there, they absolve themselves of the most unimaginable acts of cruelty.

Yet the imagined good, even when attained, still remains imaginary, just as an image of a man remains only an image. This good is false, hollow, sterile, analogous to the pleasures of a man-made paradise which lead to irremediable degradation. Here as in other instances the only courageous decision to be made is to prepare for a future while conserving whatever there was of the eternal in the past.

CHAPTER 4

Christianity and Modern Civilization

W E HAVE IDENTIFIED THREE SIGNS of the decline of a civilization: the disjunction between spirit and life, the conflict between the political and the social, and the prestige of collectivizing technology. These have continued to affect Christianity profoundly, to the degree that it shares in the ups and downs of history through its members.

This influence is manifested in two ways. In the first place, in the sphere of influence of what is called modern civilization, Christianity automatically experiences a decline. In the second place, the morbid microbes spread by civilization in its death throes make their way into the lives of most Christians, warping their minds and transforming their reactions to the world and to God. In the first case, modern civilization stifles the possibilities for the growth of Christianity in the hearts of people. It eliminates Christianity and establishes in its place a "humanism" which sees itself as human, nothing but human, that is, subhuman. In the second case, it corrupts the meaning of Christianity, makes the Christian faith seem like a pathological preference, and on the basis of syncretism, merges the world it is constructing with a new Christianity, emptied of its age-old substance. We will analyze each of these two phenomena in turn.

THE ANTI-RELIGIOUS CHARACTER OF MODERN CIVILIZATION

If we except the regions which the rationalist civilization of our times has not yet compromised, Christianity stagnates everywhere, declining or even dying in human societies. Where the mass man comes into being, Christianity becomes anemic and disappears. It suffices to look at the vast agglomerations which are the product of industrialism to become convinced of this. In the face of this great leprosy which spreads without stopping, we have the appalling impression that the Lord is going back to the politics of Noah's ark, according to the powerful expression of Father Doncoeur. [1]

The religious crisis is clearly contemporaneous with rationalist civilization, and coincides geographically with it. This is much more than a mere coincidence.

The key characteristic of modern rationalism is to make man disincarnate, to separate spirit and life in him. The stench which emanates from it thanks to technicism and politics with as collective a dimension as possible enters into him through all his pores, making him incapable of enduring the least measure of the leaven of Christianity. Man formed by contemporary civilization automatically refuses to be grafted onto Christianity. He has become ill-disposed to receive the message of the Incarnation which the Christian faith proposes to him, since his inborn aptitude for receiving it has been radically undermined. The failure to evangelize the masses is an obvious fact, despite the work and holiness of those who have generously undertaken this enterprise. There is a historical antecedent: Christianity did not make inroads into the Roman masses given over to the entertainment of the circus games and subject to the upheavals of the Empire in distress, though it was in the fullness of its youth, with its drive to conquer.

The reason for this lack of success is obvious to us. One of the clearest consequences of the devitalization of the spirit and the despiritualization of life, both caused by rationalism, is the loss of an ontological sense of the real, in particular of the manifestation of the real which is closest

---

1   Father Paul Doncoeur, 1880-1961, French Jesuit, author of numerous works on the spiritual life, art, and history.

to us: our neighbor himself. Mass man, as such, is literally inaccessible, unless the last remaining reflex reaction of his weakened vitality is stimulated: that of self-conservation and self-defense, which clearly puts him in opposition to his fellow man. His disembodied spirit, uprooted from life and also from social groups, family, trade and profession, and homeland, proves itself defenseless before collectivist ideologies and techniques which pander to his inborn propensity to engage in conflict and which seem to him like a substitute for salvation. To the degree to which he vaguely longs to be saved, his uprootedness turns him away from what is real and forces him to create out of nothing the ideologies and techniques which he will then be content to orchestrate and systematize, under skillful leaders, in order to engage his last defensive reflex reactions against death. This is undoubtedly the basic flaw in "bourgeois" liberalism and in socialism, to have been ignorant about the incarnate condition of man and his organic bonds with reality, ignorance which has worked in favor of their own victory.

Having lost a sense of reality and human connectedness, but obligated to live side by side with his fellows, man then takes refuge in an imaginary representation of his social existence, which establishes itself as an absolute for him since it maintains his self-image, with its illusory freedom from all structures, all constraints, and which is however the opposite of an absolute because it is unreal. His atheism like his degraded faith, his "mysticism" – which, like what he denies, involves different degrees, from ritual gestures associated with a minimal participation, to a faith-inspired vision – derive directly from this.

This is because the collective, in the measure to which it is collective, does not think, does not feel, experiences no affective impulse towards others or towards what lies beyond it. Only a personal being whom a spirit incarnates and gives life to and who, in life, perceives the transcendence of what is real, is capable of thinking, feeling, and loving. A man who is identified with the collective is reduced to a mechanical device operated from without, where the least idea of God is banned. If it springs up, it is similar to the seed fallen on rocky soil, where it cannot penetrate to the sphere of the social life. It unfailingly dies. It is only in a being with a soul not separated from life in whom the idea of God can become an intuition, a kind of obscure impulse coming from the ontological reality of the absolute, since in that case the concept of God finds in the soul ground which has already been worked by concrete earthly examples of the transcendent which it has encountered.

This is why man whose existence is absorbed into the collective is struck with blindness as soon as he is presented with the concept of God, and a fortiori, of Christ, God incarnated into earthly existence. Man's imprisonment within himself here below, with no way to raise his sights on high, makes him an atheist for whom God has no meaning.

The word "God" repels him, as he can only believe in a collective pseudo-existence, which greatly consoles him in his weakened state. We are dealing with the great mystery of religious atheism here. The man who believes in nothing has certainly never existed, even before the preaching of the Gospel. To believe is essentially to adhere to something which cannot be seen, but which exists beyond our understanding. Faith is consubstantial to man, because he is not all in all. Yet in disincarnate man, belief bounds in one leap to the imaginary universal collective, with his mind serving as a vehicle, to which he holds all the more firmly given that it is fused with his very self. The collective is at once he himself and like God, what is beyond himself. Without this leap into the collective, shoulder to shoulder with the herd, in which his weakness is multiplied and disguised as power, he would be mercilessly pushed out of a world where there remain for him only infinitesimal possibilities for integration. He must find the world from which he has been uprooted: he must live. The only sense of the divine which he still has is that of a debased pantheism which is summed up as the possession of the world by means of the imaginary collectivity of which he is a member, as he can no longer exist in a world that belongs to him: his disembodiment has expelled him from it. He holds on to atheistic collectivism like a lifeline. The collectivity stands before him as the mediator of existence, like Christ, but of an existence exclusively geared to the earth where he must live. His pantheism is joined to a radical materialism.

Thus in the ambience of modern civilization man evolves in a downward direction, away from Christianity. He is incapable of conceiving a personal non-material God who becomes incarnate for the salvation of men. For him to grasp this, the evangelist must make him climb back up the slope which he has descended. The foundation for belief in God has collapsed within him: there remain only chasms that he can climb out of, with difficulty, in exceptional cases. Any remaining imperceptible movements towards the transcendent are seen and judged only by God.

As bitter as this observation may be, we arrive at the conclusion that the man given over to the seduction of present civilization can only be made fit for Christianity if he escapes from the deleterious influences he undergoes. Yet nothing allows us to predict that this will happen. Just as at the end of an ancient civilization, but in an incomparably more profound and universal manner, modern man appears to be in tune with the civilization which he has built; an unimaginable catastrophe must occur in order to create a rupture in that sinister complicity. When we consider with what avidity, exaltation, or resigned astonishment man accepts rationalist ideas which fill his arid mind and glut his animal instincts, we must agree that these ideas are the projection of his most intimate being and that he wholly recognizes himself in them.

It is especially difficult for Christianity to survive in this climate given that its supporting ideology is articulated in three concepts directly opposed to the dynamism of the Christian message: the idea of progress, the spell of technology, and the obsession with politics.

THE IDEA OF PROGRESS

The idea of progress which has seized the world since the eighteenth century, captivating the imagination of our contemporaries despite the many events which sounded severe warnings, is the direct product of the disjunction between spirit and life. It arises everywhere as soon as organic relationships among people are broken, and as a consequence it constitutes an unmistakable index of decline. History bears witness to this: we find it in its pure state in the escapist myths, detached from everyday reality, which Eastern religions propagated when ancient civilization was in decline.

The idea of progress detaches man even more from his roots. Since his soul is devitalized, without the warmth of contact with what is natural and fosters his integration into life, his only recourse is to identify with a spirit, a collective mind or a sort of cosmic spirituality, in which each person bathes as though in a regenerating plasma. It is very difficult for man to lose his soul irredeemably. We always transform what we have lost, seeking it in an exaggerated form, a caricature, giving it an existence reinforced with empty contributions from our imagination. This law is verified in every area. What was confounded with the self and limited by it is magnified infinitely from without, like a circle which breaks open and releases a tangent which goes off in a straight line without stopping. Also, when the spirit becomes disembodied under the force of devitalization, it expands into a soul of the world in which the concepts of man in the Age of Enlightenment, the Hegelian ideology, the Marxist ideology, and the myth of universal communism represent the successive stages. Since this spirit or collective mind is only an abstraction, it is unlimited by space and time. Human consciousness, coextensive with the world, then comes to take on the status of something divine.

Such dreams would not have any significance if they did not determine behavior. In fact, we never lose anything: our energies are conserved and transformed. The lie is the product of the breakdown of the truth, but it in turn aspires to be the truth. Our zeal to pursue what is authentic always shifts to what is inauthentic. The concept of the collective which spawns devitalization is also called, by virtue of its very nonexistence, to inscribe itself in events and to actualize itself ever more perfectly. But it can only accomplish this by a process of negation: so that it can at last exist, it must eliminate whatever is foreign to itself. Being situated in the future, it must annihilate the legacy of the past which hinders it; it destroys anything it encounters which is not adapted to its structure. How then could the concept of the collective not be progress, since it is built on ruins? Its nonexistence constrains it to deny existence in order to exist and to reveal the constant superiority of its march forward. All progress is thus dialectical, as Marxism has aptly perceived; it implacably unfolds by means of a series of negations. However, though not perceived by Marxism, this dialectic is only carried out in a climate of marked human devitalization.

Whence comes the strange Manichaeism which cuts across all areas of human life and which is due to the obsession to oppose what has gone before: progress and the reaction to it, science and ignorance, light and darkness, modern and ancient, fascism and anti-fascism, good and evil . . . Our times are times of purging, in one direction or another.

Since it is a pseudo-absolute which guides the devitalization of modern people, the idea of progress changes into a revolutionary nihilism which puts to death what is relative, whatever serves as an intermediary, what Plato called *metaxu*,[2] whose nature is that of a creature. Simone Weil remarks, "What is it a sacrilege to destroy? Not what is here below, since that has no importance. Not what is on high, since even if he wished to, no one could touch it. The *metaxu*. The *metaxu* form the region of good and evil. Do not deprive any human being of his *metaxu*, that is, the related, interconnected goods (home, country, traditions, culture . . .) which give warmth and nourishment to the soul and without which no human life is possible, sainthood excepted."[3] However, the idea of progress, a result of the denial of the incarnate soul, destroys the *metaxu* everywhere: it wipes out whatever might, by means of its very propensity for creating relationships and bringing together diverse elements, recall to man his creaturely condition.

It is strange to note, in this regard, the concomitant decline, under the influence of the idea of progress, of social bodies intervening between the individual and the state, of intermediaries between man and what is real which provide a moral code (traditions, customs, proverbs, intuitive knowledge of nature, age-old wisdom), of intermediaries creating affective bonds between people and God (religions, cults, churches), of intermediaries intervening in male-female relationships (parents, children, families), of basic technical methods serving as intermediaries connecting human work and objects, and so many more. The abstract concept of progress is expressed in a massive denial of natural, spontaneous ties among people. It abolishes the meaning of nature, of the neighbor, of the *coesse*[4] which brings together the innumerable relationships in the world. This is why it professes itself to be inevitable, certain: the

---

2 Greek, between. See for example Plato's *Symposium* (202d–e), in which one character defines Eros as a daimon, or divine spirit, a bridge between gods and mortals.
3 *Le pesanteur et la grâce*.
4 Latin, coexistence, with a connotation of communion.

leaf detached from the tree, subject to the force of the wind, has the same fate. This leads to the current belief that progress is only to be found at the level of mechanization. However, it also undermines man's innate sense of a Creator. As it aims to be the unalloyed good, continually denying the *metaxu*, it replaces God. It is the concept of atheism par excellence, always transcending itself without ever coming to completion, and, as a caricature of the infinite, never ceasing to manifest its automatism. If man is the future of man, and is only defined as surpassing himself over time, God is useless, inconceivable, nonexistent. This is the recurring position of the old classical atheism where a being is identified with its own past: atoms, matter, money, social standing . . . Where man is absorbed into time, the eternal is no more.

The opposite of ancient atheism, which relies on the pseudo-stability of the material aspect of nature and has something solid, substantial, well-defined in its doctrine as well as in its customs, which witness to a strength which still characterizes it, the atheistic idea of progress is essentially defined as something vague, impersonal, what modern man calls freedom, that is, the absence of delineation or specific direction in his initiatives. Under its influence, we see our contemporaries reject any limitation as an attack on this indeterminacy, which they cultivate since it corresponds to their devitalization, to their loss of contact with the ontological basis of their being and its limits. Whence comes the tendency associated with progress to denigrate, and to break faith, undoubtedly the most profound trait of the ideology of progress. Progress says "no" to whatever circumscribes and stabilizes it. It discredits substantive ties which man has to himself, other persons, and things, as soon as they are observed. Every personal attachment would be an indication of slavery or, if it has materialized, it would always be seen through the lens of an abstract concept — sex, nation, race, party, where the self is located.

Man obsessed by the idea of progress no longer manages to remember the earlier stages of his evolution. He beclouds his past with forgetfulness, since memory is determinative. The cruel character of progress and its blind indifference to its actions and their consequences derives from this. "This is the way things go, this is progress!", such is its justification. Thus progress goes from indeterminacy to indeterminacy towards an abstract universalism where actions which wreak havoc bear upon personal responsibility first and foremost. In our world, given over to progress, each person absolves himself of responsibility, each encloses himself in a web of convictions which transfer obligations arising from personal acts to the anonymous collective. The disappearance of consciousness of personal misdeeds, moral sanctions, and remorse is not surprising. The action precedes the man, who is not encumbered with its consequences. This is also why increased progress is accompanied by the obliteration of the concept of original sin, which determines what the human being is from the moment he comes into the world.

This is the paradox. Man shaped by progress, rejecting all divine and natural prescriptions, cannot regard the world around him, in which he must live, as something indeterminate. From the concrete viewpoint of action, the world appears to us as resembling ourselves: shallow, if we are shallow, profound if our soul is profound . . . If a man is weak, he abandons himself to current trends, mimicking them in their ebb and flow, their changing colors, the multiple impressions they leave. This is the story of the majority of people held captive by whatever is in style, by advertising, by political discourse . . . If a man is strong and domineering, he will impose his own way of acting, and his desires and ideas on the world. The world, people, and things will be no more for him than a field for experimentation similar to the prime matter of the scholastics, indifferent to whatever form this might take, having no depth of being. In both cases, we are faced with a materialism quite different from the old materialism, which could be termed Rabelaisian, 5 where unchanging earthly goods are sought and enjoyed in their unchanging earthly nature. On the other hand, the materialism promoted by the idea of progress makes earthly goods something fluid and plastic: it endows them with forms quite removed from their primitive nature, giving them an elusive, cerebral aspect. The sight of big cities is evocative of this. Matter is no longer taken as it is in its obvious substantiality, along with its physical limitations, but as transcending as it were its own configurations and given an amorphous character, which human artifice takes hold of in order to give it the most variable forms. The opposite of ordinary materialism, which consumes only bodily life, leaving the spirit intact, contemporary materialism sucks the blood out of body and spirit at the same time. This is no longer a materialism from which man could free himself because he is not entirely absorbed in it. It is a new materialism, unknown in previous ages, into which man throws himself body and soul, and which leaves him with no way out; it keeps referring him back to the series of self-representations which he creates.

From the religious point of view, such a situation is grave, since it changes the upward movement of man towards God into a downward movement towards the demiurgic possession of the world. Physical matter still forms the being, and every being reflects the absolute Being through a kind of refraction affecting the perception of the man who looks at it. The stories of the great converts with their abundance of vitality attest to this. But what has happened to this malleable, elusive matter, whose depths the disembodied

---

5 François Rabelais, died 1553, French Renaissance humanist, physician, and priest. His works satirizing education and monastic life portrayed characters who enjoy the pleasures of life to the hilt. The term "Rabelaisian" refers to the bawdy humor and "eat, drink, and be merry" lifestyle of these characters.

man of our times penetrates in an uncontrolled fashion? How could it still reflect God, since it no longer reflects anything but the very image of the man who fashions it? How could it still bear the imprint of God, since it receives the stamp of man, in which it is wholly vested?

THE SPELL OF TECHNOLOGY

We comprehend the reductionist influence of modern civilization on Christianity, and, in general, on all religions. This influence is visible even within the civilizations which are the most distant from ours. According to a constant law of human psychology, modern civilization engenders a "religion of man" which replaces its defeated adversary. The now-deformed soul of what has been vanquished passes into the body of the conqueror and avenges its defeat by falling into superstition.

As we examine them, the phases of this process are clear. Indeed, in the measure to which his lack of rooted-ness leads him to break the nuptial pact he has made with concrete reality, man is obliged to tap his inner resources, belonging to him and no other, which will permit him to become reintegrated into the world in which he must live. His immanence gives him the imaginary impression of being intensely free, of not depending on external things at all, of possessing the ability to transform them as he pleases. Immanence thus changes into radical transcendence. However, the mind divorced from life will only be able to conceive of the world under its mechanized aspect, in keeping with his devitalization. This phenomenon is observed everywhere: for example, where woman ceases to be for man the expression of an organic relationship, she becomes an object of pleasure, and is treated as such. In place of decreasing vitality in disaccord with the flow of nature are substituted technical innovations which trans-form the primitive pact between man and nature into an exploitative enterprise which seems to further exalt human transcendence. *Nos enim sumus quodammodo fines omnium artificialium*:[6] the world of such technology is entirely oriented towards man. In reality, this transcendence, which replaces the religion of God with the religion of man, is just as illusory as the liberty which brought it into being. Man has fallen into the trap set by his own victory over nature (and over the supernatural). He finds himself defenseless before technology, which he has created and which subsequently constitutes his world, since he lacks the least organic connection to it, which could regulate it: the machine spawns more machines. Man finds himself a prisoner of his own inventions which imperiously map out the path he has to take. Technologies become enmeshed with each other, forming an autonomous body in which linkages proliferate, mimicking life and enclosing the soul of man within a circle which gets bigger but remains impassable. The myths of Prometheus and the Sorcerer's Apprentice are legends recounting adventures; they are really about slavery. Once more, the master is actually the slave. Man depends on technology, not only in order to act, but also to exist. The only way out offered to the slave to disguise his own condition is the idolatry of the tyrant to whom he belongs. There are innumerable examples of man's adoration of technology, from those that are of the most naive to its very subtle resonance in the very depths of the mind which pretends to be detached from it. Contemporary man believes technology to be omnipresent, just as his remote ancestors believed their gods to be. He holds on to it because it has him in its grasp. He is connected to it and it is connected to him. It is a loop circuit. Natural religion is replaced by a sham religion to which each person offers sacrifice with a conscience all the more lighthearted and innocent since each offers sacrifice to himself.

---

6 Latin, we are in some way the end of everything that is made by man, St. Thomas Aquinas, *Commentary on Aristotle's Physics*.

This is indeed a very serious matter for Christianity. When knowledge of technology becomes knowledge of oneself and of the world, it is all too obvious that the very mystery of being evaporates. We are clearly aware only of what we do: there remains not the slightest enigma, the least trace of the whys and wherefores, in this thriving technology. The consonance between being and knowing is perfect, within this deceit. There is nothing beyond this world. When the natural is swept away, the supernatural disappears.

It is, however, resurrected under the form of superstition relating to the self. No paganizing superstition is as fundamentally dangerous to Christianity, even if it is anthropomorphic, since it nevertheless points man to what is beyond him. Technological magic, on the contrary, refers everything back to man: a click of a button, and the world is present to man, and man to the world. For one who possesses technology, one thing produces another automatically, there is no more to it than that: the expected result appears. This "symbiosis" between the world of technology and the world of man, each effortlessly at the disposal the other, gives rise to enormous expectations buried in the unconscious, completely determinative for the behavior of the person: security, comfort, health, accelerated progress, ease in accomplishment, within reach of the rich and to be hoped for by others via a revolution, all without expending intellectual energy. How could man not be persuaded by all this which is due him? Why not render to himself a kind of superstitious worship? Beginning with that moment, the Christian God is dead to human consciousness, because He is by essence Someone who is not owed to man, but rather Someone who gives Himself through grace. In the world of technology, we see the shrinking sphere where happiness, fulfillment, the flow of intellectual energy (and physical, even if not appropriately channeled) lead to God. The sphere where unhappiness, suffering, uncertainty, and weakness are found also contracts, since technology is designed to eliminate it. Man alone rules, the slave of a slave, the tyrant of a tyrant, at once feeble and tough, stifling grace or rejecting it.

THE OBSESSION WITH POLITICS

Contrary to what occurred in former civilizations, the religious principle which up to now has governed all other cultures, under whatever form, coarse or refined, natural or supernatural, is replaced here by the political principle, itself arisen from a secular anti-religious virus which appears for the first time in history.

Devitalization not only diminishes man's capacity for communion with the cosmos, it also weakens his ability to participate in the common good. People today are no longer susceptible to being connected organically to their fellow man by a kind of summons, indefinable like everything which arises from life, which impels them to go beyond themselves towards a lived social situation where their individuality endures. They no longer embrace relationships between one concrete being and another which life continually establishes in social bodies. These are now established within a shared discontinuity which brings people together as a function of their common insufficiency. They become vaguely aware of their social exhaustion and gather together within this awareness. As we saw earlier, the collective then takes the place of the social. Ramuz writes, "Men today deny their families which are their own flesh and blood, and they deny even their own flesh, as they have suffered because of it. They look for like-minded brothers beyond geographical borders, and no longer see themselves in those around them. They want brothers who have the same ideas, and put their hopes in an abstract kinship. They take refuge in the world of ideas out of fear of and distaste for reality. They fail to acknowledge any notion of native soil and any kind of attachment of flesh and blood as though their thought developed out of itself and was nourished from its own resources."[7]

Once basic social relations have disappeared, man finds himself alone. He is no more than an "I". Politics must weave artificial bonds between him and others aimed at making them into a coherent body. In other words, politics is called to completely reestablish man in his person and in his relationships just as grace does: it mimics the presence of God in the soul of the Christian and in the Mystical Body which forms the assembly of the baptized. People today cling to the political as to the transcendent, which it caricatures. They do this all the more easily as the political merges with their own self: being no more than an idea, it only exists in their imagination. Politics thus must exclude Christianity from the arena of human life for which it is its competitor. The true religion is henceforth political ideology. There is no other which can grant salvation to man. Through an unfortunate coincidence politics has at its disposal the appropriate means for taking charge of people, in the internal forum as much as in the external forum, like God Himself. Again we ask, how could Christianity continue alongside this?

The conclusion we have reached on this point will be briefly expressed. The governing norms of contemporary civilization, the idea of progress, technology, and political ideology undermine all the conditions propitious for the development of the *anima naturaliter christiana*[8] or are radically opposed to Christianity. Today the Christian seed falls on rocky soil. As Chateaubriand had foreseen, "the time of the desert is returning; Christianity begins again in the barrenness of the Thebaid, in the midst of a formidable idolatry, the man's idolatry of himself."[9]

---

7   *Chant de notre Rhône*, 1920.
8   Latin, the naturally Christian soul, an expression used by Tertullian to refer to the predisposition of the pagan to Christianity.
9   François-René de Chateaubriand, 1768–1848, French writer, historian, and politician, *Mémoires d'outre-tombe*, 1849–1850. The Thebaid refers to

THE INFLUENCE OF RATIONALISM ON
THE CHRISTIAN WAY OF LIFE

The mysterious signs announcing the decline of civilization run through the lives of a good many Christians. This phenomenon is not at all surprising: no one escapes an environment so saturated with it. We are thus going to find in the mentality of Christians today the divide between spirit and life characteristic of our age. The first Fathers of the Church likewise drew attention to the continuing influence of the morals of their time on their coreligionists. Clement of Alexandria wrote of them: "They are like polyps which attach themselves to rocks and take on the color of the stones they adhere to".[10]

For several centuries, and in our times with a dizzying speed, the rationalist virus has infiltrated the lives of Christians and influenced how they conduct themselves towards God and creation. It has given up on weakening the Church as intermediary between the Christian and God with her inspiration, doctrine, sacraments, and structure, which remain intact. The times of the great heresies which made a frontal attack on the essence of Christianity appear to be over. The last of them, so aptly called modernism, aimed less at doctrine itself than at the attitude of the Christian before God and the world. It attacked the manner of believing rather than belief. It changed the orientation of the faith more than the faith itself. It poisoned the river at its source rather than in its course or at its mouth.

The phenomenon of modernism is revealing. It means that the enemy has changed strategies. It is from now on the members of the Church, Christians themselves, whom it threatens. It no longer assaults the house, as it did before, in order to transform it. In an imperceptible way it attacks

---

a desert in southern Egypt where a number of Christian hermits lived around the fifth century.
10   Clement of Alexandria, d. 215, theologian and philosopher regarded as a Church Father.

the residents themselves, who, enveloped in its invisible presence, take on that job.

The split between spirit and life, the dismantling of the foundations of natural religion which follows, the weakening of the intuitive sense of the presence of God in the universe, the rupture of organic bonds between the creature and creation, all these related factors tend to corrupt the man who is Christian and thus to engulf Christianity within the decline of the civilization.

If Christianity is defined as a relationship sui generis between nature and the supernatural, the result of this process would be to change the structure of this relationship by changing one of its subjects. To restore equilibrium, the Christian will have no other recourse than to make for himself a devalued Christianity which corresponds to the devaluation of his being, or even better, he will be persuaded, taking the opposite tack, that this transformation is not at all negative and constitutes a new phase in the history of the human spirit and of the dominion of God over nature. In the first case, balance is reestablished from below, in the second, from above. For the lack of a more appropriate terminology, we will designate as "bourgeois" the first form of contemporary Christianity and as "historical" or "progressive" the second.

"BOURGEOIS" CHRISTIANITY

The original form of bourgeois Christianity is indisputably Jansenism. The exaltation of the individual which to all appearances characterizes it should not give us any illusions. If the bourgeois Jansenist only believes in a supernatural God, infinitely far from the world of man's activity, it is above all because he no longer believes in the natural, in a natural religion, or the mysterious conjunction of forces governing the universe. The astonishing accuracy of this psychological insight, which Jansenism confirms, presupposes, moreover, that the evil which he denounces with such certainty is present in him. If he puts the natural and the supernatural into separate airtight compartments, it is because he sees within himself that they are mutually repugnant to each other. Grace no longer has any roots in man, and for him Christianity takes on a discarnate, ascetic, and pallid countenance, already heralding his later devitalization. By preserving his faith from all contacts with nature and its emotional resonance, the Jansenist introduces into it the leaven of rationalism, a prelude to its decline. His theology, governed by a rigorous series of clear, harsh, and incisive propositions, setting up a fierce antithesis between creation and the Creator which makes God into an implacable geometrician, shows that in it the spirit has consummated its rupture with life. The orthopedic apparatus girding his religion is an indication of congenital deficiency: he presents himself as a spectacle of the lack of vitality overcompensated by a rigorism which is conceptualized more than lived. In short, Jansenist Christianity surges, so to speak, from the confines of being to the superior spheres of speculation where it shuts itself up and imprisons in itself man and his way of life. It is in this sense the preliminary sketch of radical formalism, which is its last embodiment.

Nothing is more opposed to the Jansenist form of Christianity than the peasant Christianity of Péguy, nourished with sap coming from creation:

> The tree of grace and the tree of nature
> Have joined their trunks together with such solemn bonds,
> They have so entwined their fraternal destinies
> That they have the same essence and the same stature. [11]

To the degree that it was untenable (for the Christian life is itself organic and made up of relationships), this phase of bourgeois Christianity was rapidly transformed into deist belief. Its God, abstracted from the concrete

---

11 *Eve*, 1913.

world, developed by the human being given over to living abstracted from life in order to make his ascetic thought a summation of himself, has degenerated into an impersonal concept, the algebraic template of which is supplied by laws concerning the material, discovered and formulated concurrently. The God of the Voltairean bourgeois comes to the scene, reigning but not governing, of such transcendence that it is now no longer perceived, who lets the world below evolve in total liberty. Let us recall, then, the words of Bayle: deism is close to atheism.[12]

Between these two extremes is situated the particular form taken by the bourgeois Christianity of our age. While it has endless variants and is nearly always made up of subtle psychological gradations, we can easily make out the characteristics shared by every religion in its decline, contaminated by the ambient civilization: the disincarnation of God and man, the transfer of divine and human values into the sphere of the impersonal, the schism between spirit and life, and the increasing compartmentalization of the supernatural and the natural, now in separate categories.

The relations between Christians and God are barely personal, inimical to any total, visible integration. They are established at the cerebral level without penetrating to and fertilizing the origins of action. Divine reality is considered here as an abstract principle, like an overriding law relating to order, in particular to social order, itself impersonal, juridical, contractual, with the possibility of mechanization lying in wait. Christ rather than seen as a person of the Holy Trinity become incarnate for the salvation of the human race becomes a watered-down, hazy image, bloodless, unreal, evanescent. The evangelical message sees its power weaken and run dry, reduced to some moral maxims, the most preeminent of which are limited to a veneer of respectability cloaking worldly

---

12 Pierre Bayle, 1647–1706, French lexicographer and philosopher espousing skepticism. See his *Continuation des pensées diverses sur la comète*, 1705.

relationships. The Christian mystery loses its dynamic impetus. In the most favorable of cases, it proceeds from a faith termed "enlightened," that is, made as acceptable as possible to all minds, rid of any "superstitious" excrescence, secretly hostile to the intervention of God in the course of the happenings of life. Found first and foremost behind systems of thought and significant enterprises in the life of society, this faith adheres only to what is "reasonable." Most often the Christian mystery is only given a rough approximation of credence, like an imposing but external entity, hardly approached except as one might take a remedy when ill, never integrated into daily life, which devolves upon work in a world distinguished and separated from it, no longer a created world, no longer reflecting the countenance of the Creator.

Such a world no longer offers anything mysterious, frightening, obscure: the bourgeois has a clear, intelligible understanding of it, since he creates it anew each day, all around him, through his industry. Between God and the world stands man, solid, substantial, self-aware and self-content, asking God for His credentials, which give Him entry into only the surface of a mind uprooted from life, determined not to allow Him to go further. The life of the bourgeois is oriented to the profane world, the Godward dimension of his spirit is eclipsed: between the two there is no common viewpoint. His religion becomes internalized, but this internalization is the opposite of being rooted in existence. The "spiritual" religion of the bourgeois thus loses the vigor, tone, and sap which confer vitality. A God who is intelligent, thoughtful, wise, the enemy of all foolishness, a God not experienced by human beings in their lives, is what the bourgeois God tends to become. It is a God who is no longer "Thou," but a rational being. Bourgeois religion, denuded of the power to inhere in the person (or his innermost beliefs) which enables a dynamic participation in the world, consists in a "religion" of "me" with its own immanence rather than in an affective relationship with the divine transcendence.

A twofold consequence follows. First, bourgeois Christianity, devoid of its substance, denuded of the richness of the actual relationship between the "I" and the absolute "Thou," becomes impoverished and turns into a convoluted neutrality which rejects total commitment. Then it becomes mechanized into pure ritualism. Certain religious rites are clothed in ostentation, to the degree that they accompany ceremonies and external celebrations able to mask the lack of actual personal relations between man and God: baptism, marriage, funerals, which in their social character disguise the destitution of that relationship, and which, if necessary, could dispense with any personal involvement. These rites stand up better than others to the wearing effects of time and disaffection with religion. It is not the same with sacraments which require direct communion between the whole person and God: penance and the Eucharist for example. This is why devitalized Christianity puts them in second place or makes them fade from sight. In the case of these sacraments, where God cannot be transformed into an abstraction and where His presence, felt to be a necessity, must become incarnate in life, He vanishes from man's field of consciousness, which only retains what is adapted to its devitalized state: *quidquid recipitur ad modum recipientes recipitur.* [13] To this typically bourgeois phenomenon is added the distinction between belief and practice: "We're believers, but we don't practice!". In other words, belief in God does not breach the abyss which in man separates spirit from life. Belief is enclosed within an internal space which is no longer anything but a void.

This lack of the incarnation of Christianity in the bourgeoisie is key to the understanding of the dechristianization

---

13   Latin, whatever is received is received in the manner of the receiver, i.e., people only understand what they are able to, or disposed to, understand. St. Thomas Aquinas *Summa Theologiae* I, q. 75, art. 5.

of the people. It is moreover accompanied by a related detachment from the concept of one's fellow man. The ideology of the rights of man, disseminated throughout the world by the bourgeoisie, has taken the place of the actual, concrete neighbor. Whatever might have been said about this, this abstract fraternity in no way shows the presence of a degraded Christian inspiration, but rather a caricature of its devitalization. It is all too clear that a doctrine which no longer regards one's fellow man as a fellow man, living in close proximity, is situated at the antipodes of Christianity.

This separation between spirit and life on the level of relations with one's neighbor is powerfully reinforced by a new economic tool, invented by the bourgeoisie and perfected from the moment of its existence: money. It is absurd to dream of an earthly world where money would count for nothing. But it is one thing when money is put to the service of essential exchanges between one man and another, and another when money is held as the absolute means of exchange, apart from any concrete human relationship. In the first case money is made fruitful through its subordination to human values, as a plant made fruitful by the sun. The second case is a way of conceptualizing things in which man refers everything that is beyond him back to himself. Now this abstract way of thinking, detached from life, found at the origin of our industrial, commercial civilization and integrated into it, is admirably adapted to the divided mentality of the bourgeois Christian, who has reaped its benefits. It is superfluous to take this to court again, since the trial has too often been corrupted by those who bring suit through an appetite identical to the one which motivated the accused. Let us simply point out the ravages caused by money seen as an abstract, fluid commodity. It has the power to kill one's fellow man since it permits man to get along without him. "You have given me your work. I have given you your pay. We're even." Under the rule of money, the absolute means of exchange, an anonymous human being wanders aimlessly, interchangeable with any other, with no connections, who due to this fact will in turn have to pose as an absolute. In disembodying and "spiritualizing" the value of money, industrial civilization, the work of the bourgeoisie, has ruptured the living ties among people. It has contributed to the weakening of the vitality of the Christian religion in those of its representatives who have the duty of serving as examples to the people.

Moreover, the economic and social structure of the bourgeoisie offers a line of least resistance to the possibilities of a split between spirit and life continually operative in people of our time. It is a fact firmly grounded in history that the occupations of working in fields and plying trades, in close proximity to the living force of nature and based on direct exchanges between man and his neighbor, are eminently suited to the religious spirit – if they are not first disrupted by the influence of money. The reason for this is simple. Through his hands and the tools that serve as an extension of them, man puts something of himself in his work. He becomes incarnate, so to speak, in what he makes. Man, with the spirit and life which constitute him, is in an immediate relationship with what is real, the object of his work, which he no doubt dominates in a certain way, but to which he must continually respond because what is real in turn has a hold on him and inculcates in him the virtues of obedience, acceptance of what is, wisdom, and openness to all the voices of the universe: the peasant and craftsman change the world so little in comparison with what they accept of it! They stay close to the source of being and this nearness inclines them to contemplation. The religious relationship of the actual person with actual transcendence, which they feel to be present in the world, is usually forged in their hearts, as long as it is evident in their relationships in everyday life. Their faith must be embodied. Thus the countryside is a great reservoir of religious spirit in the degree to which the elites around whom society revolves maintain this spirit and make it visible.

It is not the same with specifically bourgeois occupations: industry, finance, business, at least when they, since they are on a large scale, abolish the possibility of close contact between people and things. As strong as the faith of those involved in these occupations may be, their religious influence is next to nothing, since natural channels of communication are lacking. These activities put at man's disposition powers of an impersonal nature which require the attention and presence of his disincarnate self. The extent of this varies from individual to individual, though it affects social life to a great degree, without arbitrarily reducing it into manageable abstract categories. The current of life going from man to what is real is then interrupted. Between man and being there intervene mental constructs which no longer proceed from life, which take on a mechanical dimension: management, machines, red tape, statistics, computation, where the character of the elements of the whole is annulled, where man only acts while becoming disembodied himself. It is all too clear that such an attitude is hostile to the relationship of man with God: how could one who cannot love his neighbor, whom he cannot help but see, love the God whom he does not see?

Thus where the law regarding incarnation no longer has any force, there is no longer an example for man to follow. And where the light is under a bushel, Christianity withers away and disappears. We must not be deceived: no preaching, no religious instruction, can take the place of an example. Christian values lived out in an exemplary way are and remain the only vehicle for the propagation of the faith for the majority of people. To a large degree the responsibility for the religious defection of the masses rests on the shoulders of the bourgeoisie, which is in charge of the management of modern civilization and which finds itself to be socially and religiously disincarnate.

HISTORICAL CHRISTIANITY

This phenomenon, which in our days has assumed great importance, leads us to look at the progressive form of current Christianity. Convinced that the historical role of the bourgeoisie has ended and that the coming of the masses onto the historical scene constitutes an evolution which it would be futile to oppose, a good number of Christians hope to evangelize this "fourth estate"[14] by attenuating the Christian faith as required by the tremendous task facing it. However, this is merely the external dimension of this new Christianity. As difficult as it may be to penetrate the mysteries of a developing movement where utopia and generosity are confounded together, it is still possible to discern the overall governing principles.

Contemporary civilization, we are told, is the daughter of Christianity. If it ostensibly denies its origins, it is only deceiving itself about their true meaning. Besides, since the coming of Christ, the evolution of the world is inseparable from the realization of the evangelical promises, indefectibly in process, without the least interruption, until there is only one flock and one shepherd, the universal Christ. There is nothing in the current crisis which should disturb the Christian soul. It is merely a crisis of growth, accompanied by impurity, excess, all kinds of violence, like all crises involving adaptation to a better condition. The evils we endure are the pains accompanying the birthing of a new humanity elevated to cosmic dimensions. A new society, the burden of which is borne by democracy, is slowly emerging from the caverns of history. It develops cultural, political, and economic values through science, technology, liberty, justice, progress, solidarity, and prosperity, which have as their goal the unity of the world under their banners. Thanks to a methodical organization of earthly aspirations, improving on the rough attempts of

---

14   The three estates of the Ancien Régime were the clergy, nobility, and commoners.

preceding ages, their very nature disposes them for integration into the catholicity of the Church. Their dynamic
thrust is irresistible. Humanity has laboriously invented
them in order to escape from the carapace of a past which
its advancement does not tolerate. Situated once again in
their authentic perspective, temporarily off course due to
their own exuberance, the ideals espoused by the modern mind are moreover only the refraction through time
of evangelical truths, which Christians had lost hold of
through weariness or weakness. It is thus important for
Christians today, more anxious about the ecumenism of
their faith, more aware of the humanism which is deployed
as suited to the world, to work wholeheartedly for the
social and temporal realization of the ideals which extend
the Gospel throughout the world. Their task is to reconcile
the Church with modern civilization, separated from each
other by the blind prejudices inherited from a bygone age,
in order to offer to God the world of the future in the final
stage of the ascent of humanity. Far from being threatened,
except by retrograde souls, Christianity sees vast apostolic
horizons open before her.

These theories, diffused throughout the nebula of the
neo-Christianity now in the process of formation, taking
on according to circumstances a philosophical, political,
or scientific cast, draw on the store of resources made
available. It is first of all necessary to get into our heads,
and especially into our hearts, that Christianity is not
made to rescue the masses or to promote the values of a
civilization, but to introduce into each actual human being
the yeast of grace. To conceive of Christianity as capable
of crowning the aspirations of whatever collectivity or to
baptize the ideals of modern civilization, whatever they
may be, is to lower it to the level of the various ideologies
which appear before the crowds in order to infect them
with a "new order." A subtle, insidious inferiority complex,
quite obvious, operates in neo-Christians influenced by

modern science, technology, and the philosophy of history, even politics. They respond to this by "sublimating" their own faith, and by a curious transposition of Freudianism, making grace – formerly conceived of as an "accident" by scholastic theology – the driving force and the hypostasized substance of the evolution of humanity. Christianity is only social inasmuch as it is first personal, such is the greatest truth which is important to recall to them.

What is more, the masses constitute a sociopathological phenomenon which surpasses, by its very nature, the poverty towards which the spontaneous impulse of Christian charity is directed. St. Dominic described this in a striking image, "grain that is packed together ferments," and Lamartine foresaw the consequences:

> Let man in search of himself avoid crowds.
> Let the human face be for him a joy:
> The mob colliding with itself perverts man's desires,
> And men too close to others are nasty. [15]

The task required is to do away with the phenomenon of the masses so that people instead of being packed together with their kind could re-create organic bonds which make them present to each other. The problem today, then, does not consist of a sprint race to the finish between Christianity, as augmented as it may be, and the various pseudosocial ideologies which work their attraction on the masses. It is not a matter of fighting modern civilization on its own ground, at the risk of getting bogged down in it. It is simply an issue of relieving overcrowding among the masses. Now this operation, supposing it were possible, would not be the task of Christianity as such: grace only directly transforms individuals. It would be a work of social, political, and economic healing, which is under the jurisdiction of the natural order, but for which Christianity would obviously be of the utmost help, if the operation were undertaken. For

---

15   *La chute d'un ange*, 1838, by Alphonse Marie Louis de Prat de Lamartine, 1790–1869, French lyrical poet and statesman.

while faith only incorporates the Christian into the Church, the Mystical Body of Christ, and does not insert man into a specific social body, it can improve societies, institutions, and civilization in specific ways, going through the necessary channel of individuals. To take a typical example, Christianity in no way "informs" the family, but it increases the virtue of its members and fosters a more complete cohesiveness in interfamilial interchanges. All things being equal, the members of a Christian family are closer than those of a non-Christian family. The pretense of seeing the social groups of an era in an evangelical framework (or discerning hypothetical harmony among them) stems from an error from which the best intellects of our time cannot free themselves, which consists in considering the society – whether it be healthy or ailing – as a kind of gigantic individual. Our contemporaries are literally hypnotized by the collective. The myth of the "great beast" captivates them: collective entities are in their eyes endowed with a life of their own.

Let us go back to the conclusion of the last chapter: the collective, taken as such, has no existence, except where man has degenerated. What does exist is an ensemble of persons dependent on each other by virtue of strictly natural factors where human strategies have only a secondary role: a community is then formed through their organic bonds. Consequently if a community becomes Christian, it is to the degree that it is made up of individuals who have themselves become Christian, where the freely-made relationships running through it are suffused with Christianity. The faith which permeates the personal conduct of its members cannot not affect their conduct in society. Thus we arrive at the obvious fact that a society is Christian only to the degree that its members are Christian. The more deeply Christian individual persons are, the more Christian will be the society they live in. Yet the condition sine qua non is that a society must first exist. Now the masses are not a society. They could never become Christian, no matter how holy the evangelist is. Individual conversions which might occur will never have any social influence since the converts do not dispose of interdependent relationships apt for transmitting the faith. For the masses to accept Christianity, they would have to cease to exist as a mass, and then reforge social bonds among themselves. The robust Christianity of the apostolic age did not save the decadent Roman masses. The debilitated Christianity of today will not save the masses spawned by contemporary civilization.

As for the values held by moderns, it is advisable to look at specific examples which one by one reveal their opposite: liberty, servitude; justice, vengeance; technology, economic paralysis and war; solidarity, division; greatness, partisan pettiness; prosperity, famine ... Even the universal esteem in which science is held, explicated, and disseminated among people of various mentalities only engenders a pretentious ignorance, which permeates modern man to his bones, at school, in the press, through the radio and cinema.

These values in and of themselves are not up for discussion: they are indisputably noble. What is called into question is the anthropological structure of man who receives them and debases them. As soon as we have understood the phenomenon of the current non-incarnational approach, the problem of the values termed modern, where the worst confusion reigns, becomes wondrously clear. The best nourishment becomes poisonous when digestion is compromised. The rupture of the nuptial bond between spirit and life, between man and the order of existence where his life takes root, transforms values into abstractions allocated in a mechanical fashion to a "human" material denuded of a soul, where the values change into their opposite. The devitalized soul projects them onto an amorphous "life" which is no longer nourished by the experience of what is real. With any connection to reality vitiated by the mind and by life experience, values turn into imaginary models of behavior which completely destroy what they claim to establish: imaginary nourishment eliminates real food. Thus does liberty, not embodied in the human being, its seat and overseer, reduce man to slavery by destroying the limits within which he could actually be free. Imposed on a divided being, liberty escapes through the fissures within him, carrying with it all the real kinds of freedom which he would have been able to enjoy. This kind of liberty uproots the tree, prevents the sap from flowing through its branches, and hands over its dead wood to the axe of the lumberjack. It is the same with all the other values which are in the process of unifying the planet. Their dialectical action is bringing the world towards unification by means of the emptiness which covers over the fragmentation of people, increasingly sealed off from each other, with a blanket of words. Fictitious unity and its opposite are inextricably connected: real unity is destroyed, crushed between its caricature and its negation.

It is futile to add that modern "values" understood not as values or modern, but in their relationship to the man of our time, reveal humanity's tremendous fundamental regression, analogous to that undergone by ancient civilization before succumbing to deterioration from within. Far from being in advance of Christianity, these values distance themselves from it, since an abstract, disincarnate humanity aspires to them, incapable of acting except as a mass and under the direction of agitators who consume their last reserves of vitality. To be empirically convinced of this, one has only to be present at any meeting: one will comprehend from living (or rather moribund) experience the very moment when the last energetic interventions of a people are shamelessly thrown into the blazing fire of "values," which turn them into smoke. Any truth still held by man in his weakened state is immediately destroyed by the lie of "values."

We now understand why Christianity no longer has any effect on contemporary humanity. Contrary to the idea popularized by Nietzsche, Christianity requires its followers to have the virtue of fortitude, which is essential. [16] It is not a religion for the weak, delicate, and underdeveloped, who encapsulate their impoverished egoism within a counterfeit supernatural shell. It is the religion of those who hold out against moral corruption. If strength is the principle of human acts, as it is of nature – the forces of nature! – there is a tacit harmony between it and grace. If like everyone else the Christian falls, it is by going headlong against the moral law, and not by constructing a system of values designed to make the universe in harmony with his failure. In this sense, the sin of the strong offers more possibilities than the virtue of the weak. The progress of Christianity in the barbarian world of the past and its decline in today's "virtuous" world have no other explanation. Clovis was a sinner; Robespierre was "virtuous"; let us take stock of the difference. [17]

Here is what a certain sector of the Christian intelligentsia no longer understands, sheltered in its supernaturalism, in its ignorance of the nuptial pact man has made with nature, in the forgetfulness of the actual presence of the neighbor of flesh and blood. In this regard, we recall an eminent Christian philosopher, a specialist in social and political matters, who confessed to us one day that he had never shaken hands with a worker! How many priests and religious, isolated in their seminaries and professorships, put forward at every opportunity theories on the future of civilization, on the relations between the Church and the

16   See, for example, *The Antichrist*, 1895, which depicts Christianity as a religion for the weak, with belief stemming from a broken will to live.
17   Clovis, c. 466-511, first Frankish king to unite all the Frankish tribes under one rule. While advancing the cause of orthodox Christianity, he committed some despicable acts, such as instigating murder for political purposes. Maximilien Robespierre, 1758-1794, major figure in the French Revolution, and responsible for much of the bloodshed, falling victim to it himself.

new civic order, without having the least acquaintanceship with the man in the street, today held as an "expert" in his subject matter!

It is distressing to see this outpouring of intellectualized love bogged down in the mire of abstract "values," under the pretext of promoting evangelical charity and not putting oneself outside the "current of history." For love seated in the intellect and geared to anointing contemporary values only exists where the abstract exists, that is, in the mind. As we have said elsewhere, "such a love can be deceptive, since it is alive, even extraordinarily so, yet existing only in the subject, since its object is nothing more than an idea." Here the actual person is the happenstance medium for the idea. He has only the theoretical possibility of engaging in reflection. Within this perspective, the concept of one's fellow man deteriorates. He is not seen as a neighbor, but in light of values which are being promoted. He is understood as an extension of one's mind, that is, of one's self. As paradoxical as the consequence of this may be, the neighbor is transformed into an idol, for there is only one idol, the self. We are witnessing the birth of an idolatry within the bosom of present-day Christianity, the idolatry of one's fellow man transmuted into an abstract idea.

As in any idolatry, this attitude admits of no competitors. It will divide Christians into two groups, those who are lagging behind the modern world, and those who resolutely advance in the front lines. The former, who practice the traditional common virtues, will see themselves criticized for their maladroitness, mistakes, crude initiatives, their petty self-interest, in short, for the all-too-common dross which accompanies human projects as they are brought into being. The duties of one's state which they tightly espouse are undervalued in favor of a romantic appeal to a charity which neglects earthly virtues in order to invest in a formless faceless man held as an absolute. In this regard, it has been too little noticed how indifferent neo-Christianity shows itself to the domestic and work-related virtues, to love of the land and community, where one's neighbor is understood exactly as a neighbor, in his actual, felt presence. For centuries, these simple human relations have served as a basis for the propagation of the faith. The new Christianity is concerned only with the second group of Christians. They have become aware of their dignity, freed from a bygone age, as they contribute to the rejuvenation of the Church, emphasizing the progress made by the world, which the Church through her vocation should align herself with.

This distinction among Christians is an extension of the difference which bourgeois Christianity set up between an "enlightened" faith, of which they claimed to be the torchbearers, and the "superstitious" faith of the lowly. The transition from bourgeois Christianity to progressive Christianity is in any event clear: the same phenomenon of devitalization is the connecting link, the same dialectic between opposite positions is the current that runs through it. Jansenism, deism, atheism, and neo-Christianity share a common factor which serves as a fulcrum for them: the denial of the human condition, a direct consequence of the disincarnate spirit. God in His personal capacity is evicted from nature, of which man is a part, either because nature is evil, because God is impersonal or mythical, or because the human person, alone capable of accepting God, transcends nature from the great height of his spiritual autonomy. In each case, nature falls into the hands of man, who makes of it what he pleases; the human spirit floats above it like a demigod. Nature is invested with the human genius and the idea of progress is born: how could it be otherwise since man is not a creator *ex nihilo*? Bourgeois Christianity sets itself up within this conceptualization of the world. Incapable of grasping the divine presence in nature which it has dominated through its industry, it establishes God as a protective casing for its actions, a shield which is external to its being and to the world where its work advances. Neo-Christianity emphasizes this separateness. Bourgeois Christianity extends the autonomy arrogated to itself to the realm of the spirit: man from now on goes towards God in freedom, without the least natural constraint. The human being becomes more and more spiritualized: he enters the "noosphere.[18] The values set forth by his spirit liberated from nature are so to speak Christian. From a sacralized nature to the human spirit to God, neo-Christianity has thus established a line of thought that progresses towards the divinization of man. In other words, it dissolves the chitinous crust of bourgeois Christianity.

Once again, the opacity permeating the mysterious relationship between the human being and nature explains to us how Christianity today lets itself be invaded by the powers of death active in contemporary civilization.

This inherent rupture is the beginning of all the others. Once the relationship of *coesse* between man and the world is broken, the very *esse* of the Christian is broken up into disparate elements: private and public life, faith and science, philosophy and theology, Church and state, history and providence ... The conduct of the Christian is then ruled by the Kantian distinction between the phenomenon and the noumenon, the latter driven back to within the disincarnate spirit.[19] As we read in a recent issue of a Catholic journal, "The physical world, history, the heart in its Pascalian sense, so many worlds without God ... Christians in their faith take note of this absence and expel this world from their sanctuary, the world which rejects the faith and abandons every attempt to find God there. This is where, it seems, an authentically religious meaning of

18   According to the French Jesuit scientist and philosopher Pierre Teilhard de Chardin, 1881–1955, this is the evolving sphere of human consciousness culminating in the unity of humanity in a communion of love.
19   According to Kant the phenomenon is the appearance of an object, all that can be experienced, while the noumenon is the thing itself, a reality that cannot be known.

divine transcendence exists, the rejection of false gods."
What is this "transcendence" which leaves behind the world
and man — who is, as the slightest experience reveals to us,
a being-in-the-world — if not an immanence barely camouflaged? Yet how can the human being attain to God *per ea
quae facta sunt*[20] if scientific, psychological, historical, and
sociological reductive theories show him that his intelligence and love have been victims of an illusion? Where
can he then find God, if not in the impersonal spirit of
science, as Renan discovered Him in the impersonal spirit
of humanity?[21] Here we are in the presence of the most
monstrous of idolatries, that which transforms the true
God into an idol, into a pure idea located in the depth of
the abyss of a totally disembodied spirit.

This attitude has a name, Hegelianizing hyperintellectu-
alism. Due to a scruple which is itself a sign of devitalization, the modern Christian feels himself to be powerless to
experience God in nature, organic and multi-colored. He
is afraid of feeling, because he can no longer feel, and he
can no longer feel because he is cerebralized to the core,
because he no longer exists as an indivisible being, all of
a piece, as the wonderful popular expression goes. Become
a eunuch for the sake of the world, he imagines as a result
that he has become a eunuch for the kingdom of heaven.
He lacks the undefinable knack, similar to a feeling, for
finding God in a universe clothed with sacred meaning, all
the elements of which are organically bound to each other
because it depends on God in the depth of its existence. In
his eyes such spontaneity has nothing of the appearance of
the "scientific." It is even dangerous, fetishist, pantheistic,
naturalistic. It compromises the supernatural.

The progressive Christian can no longer recuperate
through his own experience the purpose of life which many

20 Latin, through created things.
21 Joseph Ernest Renan, 1823-1892, French orientalist and historian of
religion who looked for a spiritual principle in human accomplishments.

pagans possessed. To speak in the language of Thomism, he no longer sees that grace directs his supernatural actions *suaviter et prompte*,[22] the way that the *forma substantialis*[23] governs his natural actions. He no longer perceives the analogy that St. Thomas discerned between creation and the influx of grace. He no longer possesses the potential for obedience, he is deprived of the self-possessed docility of his life as influenced by the influx of the divine, because life is dying within him. How would he then dare, in this century of enlightenment, to affirm the presence of God in nature and history, since people break down matter and are equipped with sufficient technological means to influence the course of events as they see fit?

This is the crux of the matter, when all is said and done: the secret fear, disguised as audaciousness, of others and what they think, the fear of not belonging to one's times camouflaged as a new momentum in the Church, the fear of being seen as dull, the loss of the sense of the actual presence of God and His transformation into an abstract entity walled off in an inner recess of the spirit, the breakdown of the mind, the imitation of others. This is how the Christian, yielding to the pressure of civilization, gets accustomed to experiencing God in his soul, in an invisible recess of his mind, giving up the rest to an intensified rationalization. He ignores the fact that what is intellectual is itself bound to the flesh and allows himself to be affected by the complete breakdown of the mind which is the secular mentality.

Not long ago Étienne Gilson[24] wrote, "What is the greatest praise that many among us can hope for? The greatest that the world gives them: 'He is a Catholic, but he's really quite all right. You wouldn't believe it of him.' Shouldn't we want just the opposite? Not to be Catholics who wear their

---

22 Latin, gently and readily.
23 Latin, substantive form, or essence.
24 1884-1978, French philosopher and historian of philosophy, specializing in medieval philosophy and the thinking of Descartes.

faith like a cockade on their hat, [25] but who so succeed in expressing their Catholicism in their lives and day-to-day work that the unbeliever comes to wonder what secret force inspires this soul, this life, and who after discovering it, says to himself what is the opposite, 'This is a very fine man and now I know why, it's because he is Catholic.'"[26]

---

25   The cockade in France is a knot of ribbons signifying allegiance to an organization, for example a political party or military unit.
26   From "L'intelligence au service du Christ-Roi" in *Christianisme et philosophie*, 1936, where Gilson writes about the transforming power of Catholicism in the lives of individuals.

CONCLUSION

NOW AT THE END OF THIS STUDY, WE feel crushed by the horizon of the future inexorably closing in on us. Questions are coming up on all sides which have only one answer: the process of devitalization is continuing without a break. Starting from a certain degree of uprootedness, man can only be explained in one way: physical causality and its statistical determination. Any unforeseen fresh starts in life are ruled out. The original bond between man and the world has been abrogated. This has consequences, as precise as those following from a series of theorems. The cycle of one civilization is coming to an end and another is already beginning, though it can in no way be perceived, for the beginnings of civilizations are similar to those of humans: they are hidden in the womb of history before being born in broad daylight.

We are all in the situation of the old man who knows that he is going to die and who cannot accept it. Like him we hold onto vain reasons for our continued existence, as though these could prolong our life, and we cast a blind eye to what will never disappear. For civilizations as for the majority of people in their declining years, the incidental takes the place of the essential: technology and liberty today, and honor and plighted troth yesterday, have the incomparable significance of an obsessive memory. What will remain of all this? A lot? A little? Nothing? The future is mute.

Besides, all that has no importance. Must we, at all costs, turn towards the "new man"? Here he is, on the scene: the sight of him is unmistakable. His features are coarse, undoubtedly a sign of future refinement. He has suffered in the inferno of history. Since he is newly arrived, and since he is distressed, he is innocent. An unstoppable movement thrusts him onto the world scene. He undermines the heritage of centuries, but in his youthful fervor he will set it right again.

We must respond, "What do we know about this?" What is new is only too often the old in disguise. What is new and only too visible is never the new which endures and promotes the eternal. Because it is all too obvious, everyone rushes to meet it and the great herd with its brute force topples it over. The new thus takes on the character of a physical force which automatically carries the world along, throwing it off balance, without the least renewal of vitality. Mimicking what is new and ostentatious is a well-known phenomenon which keeps up failing energy, though without any influx of vigor.

It is important to resist this conservatism concerning what is new with the joyous, calm confidence of the warrior who will never see the victory. The tragedy of our times is really something of limited duration. For the worshipers of progress, the experience and awareness of triumph is a necessary consolation: without it they hand themselves over to the sweep of a destiny which dehumanizes them, carrying them off to the realm of the imagination. They need to see their dream implemented on earth, right away, for fear that the lie which they dimly sense will reveal itself to be a reality. However, the dream which gives the most vivid illusion of what is real is called a nightmare.

People today must not give in to the present temptation, not only because the death and birth of a civilization go beyond a human lifespan, but for a more profound reason, one which, it must be said, is *metaphysical*, in other words, hidden, unobtrusive, imperceptible. With regard to a nascent civilization, the immediate present has no metaphysical dimension: it presents itself as a gigantic figure, compelling, captivating, without which man could never be saved. The old structures of existence buckle. To all appearances, humanity is no longer sustained by anything other than the desire to escape from the distress of this collapse. Those who take part in dismantling the structures, those who depend on them as parasites, and those who take no notice of them are in the same situation: their material existence is at stake. Their obsession grows along with the strategies – which are also material – which intervene to eliminate this state. Human existence is totally caught up in a material representation of man, all the more attractive given that it seems possible to manipulate it with ease. What is new arises in turn in the same manner, inscribing its features on to the same image in which man recognizes himself. The power of the illusion is such that thought yields to it, giving up its true function, and rejecting its incarnate metaphysical status.

Only one thing, however, remains, under the form of an infinitely reduced metaphysics, of the Leibnizian monad with neither door nor window, of the mustard seed buried in the depths of the mind: the unvarying relationship of man with the world, the basis of every civilization. [1] Whether man is diminished or aggrandized in the cycle of the civilization which is beginning, this relationship remains and it alone is necessary since it is permanent, independent of the duration of the civilization. Nothing reveals it plainly or translates it into a formula. It can only be grasped by the mind which sees it as it is embodied in the day-to-day conduct of man. If we want at all costs to give it expression, we would have recourse to the concept of harmony, to the equilibrium of the Greeks. Between man and the world, a still, vibrant harmony, barely noticeable, shifts the balance towards the pure dimension of verticality. Again, as the Greeks have shown, harmony is impossible without a kind of equality of love, mysterious in the extreme, between man and the world, without the presence in each of them of a divine spark: "Everything is

---

1 Gottfried Wilhelm Leibniz, 1646-1716, German philosopher and mathematician. He believed that every human and animal body has one dominant substance, or monad, which controls the others within it. See his *The Monadology*, 1714.

full of gods."[2] Only the thought of the cosmic, in which they both participate, can prevent human pride from dominating the world and man from being crushed by its weight. A quite elementary metaphysics is seen in the original pact between the two components of civilization which annuls any possible disequilibrium by placing the same divine weight on both sides of the scale. As with every profound dimension of reality, it is impossible to express other than by symbols, and the complete disappearance of symbolic thought in our age, blighted by slogans, makes this undertaking difficult.

The civilization which we must prepare for will be built on this infinitesimal metaphysical element. This means that activities and people who appear to be the least robust, the closest to nature, will have a vital role to play in this long-term project: the elite on the one hand, and the religious spirit on the other, in other words a kind of "nobility" and "clergy," the former rooted in the existence of man, the latter transfiguring him through contemplation, exercising an influence that in our blindness we underestimate. Moreover, no true civilization can do without a religion or an elite. The civilization providing the scenario and these others serving as actors are entrusted with the cornerstone, with the living grain of sand which sustains the whole foundation.

How then can we recover the "secret strength" which Étienne Gilson spoke of, which Christianity has lost in the eyes of most people? Is it even possible to get it back? It seems as though Christianity is condemned to lose ground – temporarily, because it possesses the promise of eternal life. We are witnessing the rise of a new paganism, infinitely worse than the ancient variety, which debases the religious

2   Ascribed to Thales, c. 626/623-c. 548/545 BC, regarded by many as the first Greek philosopher.

spirit by turning it into the idolatry of man. Every nature develops in an upward direction, though it may be on a very low level. Christianity came to elevate this tendency, which is always weakening. Since the advent of Christ, it is no longer permitted to nature to weaken without descending below its proper level. It has only one way to proceed: upwards. Paganism before Christ is one thing, a rough preparation for the Good News, as witnessed by the soul of Virgil, and another that of today, with the simultaneous corruption of nature and the evangelical message as the current doctrines of an ideological salvation attest. The former was an ascent, and the latter is nothing but a fall.

When we look at the overall problem, we must admit that no response is possible: our actions, as authentically Christian as they may be, can have no bearing on the situation as a whole. The totality of human existence is undermined today. Christian life is in fact entwined with human existence today, and suffers the inevitable consequences of this. Only God can act on the situation as a whole.

It is thus important to delineate the problem in a way that is accessible to us. It is futile to want to put oneself above a fractured world in the privileged situation of a God who contemplates the world and its events. The Christian lives in a world that is falling apart. He must realize this. Consequently, to connect the fate and activities of Christianity to the future of a civilization which is in the process of dying seems to us to be the most serious error a Christian can make. When we hear it said that Christianity alone is able to save civilization, let us not yield to the voices of sirens: this civilization is condemned because it has separated spirit and life, because it has turned away from God as it turns away from life, because it is immersed in the appalling conviction that "God is dead." The call of the world, provoking the development of ideologies, is only the fierce, destructive temptation to suicide. Christianity did not prevent the collapse of ancient civilization, even after the edict of Constantine, which permitted Christians to occupy the most important positions in the empire.

Let us note, furthermore, that Christianity finds itself in a situation incomparably more difficult than at the time of the invasion of the barbarians in the first centuries of their expansion westward, in a horizontal direction. The barbarians who overran the West had a robust vigor which the barbarians of today, who are attacking the *vertical* dimension, are quite deprived of. It was an abundantly incarnated people, overflowing with life, who bore the fragile skiff of their spirit over the waves. If the spirits of some capsized, the spirits of others continued to stay afloat, never running aground. It was enough for Christianity to calm the waters of life, as Christ calmed the raging sea. A continuity was established between the abyss of the real, the ocean, and the ship, flying the flag of grace. This task was relatively easy. It is no longer the same today. In the face of a new kind of barbarians whose spirit, separated from life, is no longer in touch with reality, Christianity proves itself to be powerless. A rupture between nature and grace is created. Nature itself is out of kilter. Christianity no longer concerns modern man, since it can only reach an incarnated person. It can no longer undertake the conquest of people in whom human nature is in the process of disappearing under the influence of a dis-incarnation, which becomes more apparent day by day. This explains the failed attempt to rechristianize the bourgeoisie and the masses by means of Catholic Action[3]: *gratia naturam supponit.* [4]

Thus the Christianity of tomorrow must first be directed to a restoration in the order of time, which corresponds to the ontological order, of the appropriate forms of life which facilitate the flourishing of man in the here and now. It is only too apparent that supernatural love cannot save what

3   Groups of lay Catholics working to influence society. Beginning in the second half of the nineteenth century, they came to include associations of workers, students, and women, and media outreach.
4   Latin, grace builds on nature.

is natural when this latter is defective. Now the man whose spirit is incarnated into life – and who thus shows himself to be capable of perceiving transcendence – comes to birth in quite specific circumstances, which a study of the history of peoples and civilizations empirically shows. We believe in this regard that the fate of Christianity depends on a recovery of social traditions, present at the origin of all civilizations. The existence of relatively small groups whose members are organically connected to each other, which facilitate awareness of the concrete presence of one's neighbor, is indispensable to the development of the religious instinct. In loving the neighbor, whom he sees, man will love God, whom he does not see. In these communities where everyday life takes place, the family, profession or trade, parish, region, country, people come together in a dynamic way since they participate in purposeful activities which transcend them, which they did not initiate and which they are in step with. These activities bring them together with other people and heighten their basic feeling of *coesse*. In this context, the family constitutes the social unit most favorable to the birth of religious intuition. By means of the constant interchanges within the family, and the hierarchy which forms its axis, it is the very image of the relationship which unites creation to the Creator. It is not by chance that all religions call God "Father", and that the Church is called the "Mother" of the faithful. It is not by chance that other social institutions, where a certain degree of intimacy among people is present, have in the past been based on this model. The converse is equally true: in the degree to which communities where everyday life takes place have been abandoned, religious sentiment has everywhere withered.

It is important, on the one hand, for Christians to get rid of their obsession with the collective, which haunts them and to which they too often yield under the pressure of an economy which places people side by side without uniting them. To let oneself be driven by the powerful economic ideologies of our time; to want to conquer through a supernatural love cut off from its end, amputated by the ideologies, which end is fellow man in the concrete; to consider that the world which has evolved towards a spirit of justice and fraternity assuring its cohesiveness but without basing it on fundamental social structures, is really to obscure what Christianity is. Without a doubt, collectivism claims to create something good on earth, free from all dross, surpassing the work undertaken by the Christian religion. But an imaginary good is nothing other than a real evil. In its realization, collectivism makes what is actually good sterile, inextricably confounded as it is with a variety of imperfections in the bosom of tutelary communities. If it slays evil, at the same stroke it eliminates what is good. It thus takes on the aspect of an absolute, turned upside down, dragging man down in its accursedness. Here one must accept a relative evil while realizing that only the love of the absolute good and a personal God can subdue it and ultimately eliminate it. To start with a "blank slate" is to be condemned to never starting out, to annihilate under the weight of the "great beast" the infinitely small metaphysics which protects the integrity of the simplest relations between man and his fellows, between man and the world.

On the other hand, Christianity itself can only survive amidst the turbulence of the present and future if it passionately holds on to the reduced number of truths which the corruption of the age has not reached and which have received, like itself, the promise of eternity. Nothing would be more harmful to Christianity than to adapt itself to the "movement of history," a constant temptation, since the movement of history, as it is cyclical, would carry it off in the infernal cycle of deaths and rebirths. One can easily imagine what would have become of Christianity if it had followed the path of the decadent Roman civilization.

On the contrary, with infallible intuition, a sign of its vitality, it bound itself to everything scorned by that dying civilization. It fearlessly turned away from the atheist "great beast" of imperial Rome; it became resolutely "anti-modern." It was rooted in man as he actually is, in the everlasting foundation of his being, beyond a historical evolution which was in the process of dissipating its last reserves, dooming them to extinction. Against ill winds and high tides, it kept before itself an awareness of human existence. It stood up against whatever removes man from his roots and subjects him to the grip of time. It has saved this infinitely small being, individual man, with his soul, his body, and the extension of his body, the milieu where he exists, his *metaxu*: home, family, country, timeless traditions, without being anxious about the salvation of the people, of the nation, race, class, or humanity. The only historical value which has ever mattered to Christianity is the past, not insofar as it is the past, but insofar as it is timeless, a lasting memory of something eternal harnessed by tradition and continually reinvigorated in the present, escaping from evolutionary cycles.

For man, extremely small, borne along in the course of time, is eternal: he transcends all of history in his soul, the principle of his life. This is where Christianity has always gotten hold of him, where the soul is joined to the body, where the soul becomes incarnate in the reality of the world which it vivifies, where it constitutes the permanent axis of every civilization. Man enters into the world to live according to the extremely demanding laws governing this relationship of the soul to the world. As tenuous as this relationship may be, Christianity will make of the man who lives within it a Christian, grafting the eternality of grace onto his own eternal destination. However, the relationship must be discovered beneath the mass of false images of himself that man endlessly fashions in order to be freed. As soon as Christianity penetrates it, the graft is successful because this particular relationship brings with it genuine vigor. At the same time, Christianity strengthens it. To take an example seen today, we will see that within several decades the family, in spite of the aberrations gravely affecting it, will have been saved by Christianity since only Christians will have adhered to the natural laws for growth, free of self-interest and artificial methods.

However, in our age that requires true heroism. To live according to nature today more than ever presupposes a strong character, and a strong character in turn presupposes the complete integration of the spirit into life. Ultimately the greatest example of character is the martyr, the most incarnate being there could be, up to his last drop of blood. This task, already bristling with difficulties at the level of the family, is even more arduous in other areas of social life. Yet we must undertake it. Our shoulders, and the shoulders of generations coming after us, must bear the crushing burden of sheer nature and grace, offered without protection, save that coming from God, against all the assaults of a mechanized civilization. This fidelity according to nature and grace to the eternal will prepare for the dawning of a new civilization and a new Christianity.

We do not, however, believe that the modern Christian can recover his "secret strength" without a huge infusion of supernatural grace. Human nature has fallen so low, its foundations have been destroyed to such a point, that it must be completely reestablished. Today we have become so weak, sunk to a such new low level, that we can do nothing without God. Everything that is happening indicates that nature must first be totally reconstituted by grace. God must first galvanize our weakening vitality before lifting it up to the heights.

In this connection, the noble figure of St. Thérèse of the Child Jesus sets out a way for us to follow. It shows no lack of respect for this saint of our times to observe how the terrain where so many virtues developed had all the

appearances of fragility. It is all too clear that her temper-
ament, compared to that of St. Teresa of Avila, for example, seemed at first glance to be lacking in vigor, almost
detached from the corporeal. Yet, below the surface, *The
Story of a Soul* reveals the life of a person of psychological
spontaneity, strength, and enlightenment which stand
out due to their character. At times a considerable effort
must be made to break through that crust, somewhat artificial, covering over grace, those garlands of "roses," that
childish facade in which the robust sanjuanist[5] message
of the saint is enfolded. This is exactly where we find the
deeply moving meaning of the invitation which the humble
Carmelite of Lisieux issues to our age and of the doctrine
of the "Little Way," which is its content: God used a being
seemingly fragile, identical in all *outward* respects to the
poor devitalized human beings we have become, in order
to propose this return to, this pilgrimage to, the natural and supernatural sources of our resurrection. For our
broken, unstable humanity, God has raised up a type of
sanctity, a great example, who to all appearances shared
the faults of the people of her age and taught them how
to overcome them.

Indeed, each age has saints which providentially respond
to its own needs. The frightening mortifications of the
desert fathers, St. Thérèse of the Child Jesus's fidelity in
little things, are teachings which introduce what is eternal
into the appropriate period. The history of sanctity and of
the specific way in which man has need of God are absolutely symmetrical. Between the overflowing vitality able
to endure the ascetic discipline of yore and St. Thérèse's
declaration "It is not necessary to perform spectacular
works, but rather to hide from the eyes of others and from
oneself,"[6] there is not the least contradiction; there is simply an *adaptation* of an identical invitation to humanity as

---

5   Referring to the doctrine of St. John of the Cross.
6   *Histoire d'une âme*, 1898. (*The Story of a Soul*).

it evolves. The exuberant nature of yesteryear needed to be greatly pruned; the anemic nature of our contemporaries needs to be continually reinvigorated root and branch. God speaks to concrete beings placed in a specific time in history, and if He demands of us the same renunciation, He does not always do this always and everywhere in the same way. There is nevertheless a constant psychological law, backed by weighty evidence, that grace has need of a nature capable of supporting the weight of heaven. St. Thérèse of the Child Jesus teaches our contemporaries to re-create their nature, to renew their energies, to fill in all the fissures opened up within them by the process of devitalization. Her apparent weakness, where an incomparable reserve of strength was stored, puts God exactly at the level of people today: "Where would your merit be if you only had to fight when you felt courageous? *What does it matter if you have no courage as long as you act as though you had!*"[7]

This is why the recovery of vitality and nature for contemporary humanity is indissolubly linked to the practice of the Theresian way. Not by pursuing an inaccessible ideal of universal moral standards, or by proposing a panacea to the world drawn up by means of abstract statements about human nature and justice encapsulated in formulas, will we succeed in rebuilding the demolished edifice of ethics. The reason for this is simple, though as yet ignored: one does not only avoid starting at the end – one does not erect a roof over clouds – but only arrives at the universal, that which is valid always and everywhere, in the degree to which the actual nature of man has been reestablished in a sufficient number of specimens. It is necessary to set solid foundations and reestablish roots. This is the only way to guarantee an elevation of the spirit which is not a flight

---

7   From the memoirs of Sister Marie of the Trinity, one of the novices under St. Thérèse's care, only excerpts of which have been published. This quotation appeared in print for the first time in the 1907 edition of *L'Histoire d'une âme*, in a section devoted to Carmelites' memories of Thérèse.

from reality, in which one falls with all one's weight into a mechanized life in order to mechanize it even more. *Qui fidelis est in minimo et in majori fidelis est.* [8]

Our eroding vitality and our human nature, which is becoming disaggregated as its elements then atrophy and harden as they engage in a relentless struggle against each other, need to be gradually put aright with incredible patience: at ground level, even beneath it, even in the unconscious, the locus of discordant psychic reflexes. The task will be of long duration, and St. Thérèse of the Child Jesus through her personal example and under the divine inspiration which led her to the Little Way, shows us how we should from now on direct our activity in the night of this new Middle Ages – marked not by an excess of strength, but by an excess of weakness – which we must live through.

Little Thérèse's lesson seems to us even more relevant on another point. She teaches us humility, and without the least paradox, what Nietzsche, the prophet, calls a return to the earth, [9] glorified by the song of the psalmist: *Veritatis de terra orta est.* [10] Regaining contact with the fertile soul which naturally exists in us is what Theresian humility means. This humility doubtlessly tends to a certain asceticism, to the restraint of our faculties intoxicated with their perfection, though it is quite relative. Yet it consists above all in the recognition, acquired through personal experience and an accurate assessment, of who we are. It is a matter of an existential humility which embraces the lineaments of our being, which patiently bears up with the concrete limits of our own reality, which refuses to escape into the void of non-being, and which, then like all that is, blossoms into joy.

---

8   Latin, He who is faithful in that which is least is also faithful in that which is greater, Luke 16:10.
9   See his *Thus Spoke Zarathustra*, 1883-1885, for the injunction to be true to the earth, since there is no hope beyond it.
10   Latin, Truth has sprung out of the earth, Psalm 85 (84):12.

Here again the method of the Little Way is masterful. In what does it consist, if not leading the individual to his *real capacity for being*, by meticulous control, not of transcendent "aspirations" which can mask his poverty, but of the multiple acts which make up everyday life? This kind of glorification of our poor earthly day-to-day activity reveals the eternal, which illuminates it. Everything happens as though the saint had intuitively perceived the essential importance of the embryonic development of existence in the atmosphere we live in, and the urgent need to protect this germ of real life which we possess and which the process of disincarnation continually puts at risk of being made sterile.

St. Thérèse discerned, with extraordinary acuity, that the reconstruction of the human person could only be fully effected within the modest requirements of everyday life here on earth. This is a warning to all the "personalists" of every stripe who crowd into the public square. There they call out for liberty and the dignity of the person, beguiling our modern reformers with their verbiage. For if man wants to save his compromised liberty, the liberty which helps him rule over the world and subjects him to self-tyranny, he must recover the concept of liberty under which his ancestors lived and which Thérèse exalts: liberty lies in the acceptance of the requirements and limits of being, not in their destruction. The teaching of St. Thérèse strikes us as inexhaustible here. In his homily for the Mass of the saint's canonization, Pius XI had already stressed: "If this way of spiritual childhood became widespread, how easily the reformation of human society could be achieved, which we proposed at the beginning of our pontificate." In this teaching is found the only theology of history which is not an imitation of Marxist philosophy of history nor an indication of an inferiority complex in the face of it.

All the Theresian doctrine is summed up as an integral realism which never loses the sense of the eternal, which is part of everything that has an authentic existence. For we have need of this realism just as we need the bread we eat. We need to live in a down-to-earth manner, in touch with Virgil's *terra justissima*, [11] which supports the weight of the heavens and is one with them. Quite removed from living in an overly earthbound fashion, under the surveillance of the Minotaur of materialism, quite removed from suffering from a lack of idealism, it is just the opposite that is true. All we do now is ignore the eminent dignity of matter: we aspire to subdue it, modify it, transform it, despite its actual nature, as a function of making ourselves into a demiurgical absolute. The law *divide ut imperes* [12] comes into full play here. This is why we are splitting apart matter under the pretext of releasing its energy, exactly as we deconstruct man under the pretext of releasing his "spiritual freedom." The complementary elements constituting the nature of a being are thus disassociated in an analytical process of increasing complexity, the end of which can be nothing but the dust of death, and we want to bring them together again, from without, in a synthesizing action which is the work of our domination over ourselves and the universe. Such an initiative involves the growing disincarnation of things and of people, as well as total disdain for their nature. The more man frees himself from the natural requirements of life in order to live "according to the spirit," the more he inserts himself into a soulless mechanical process that requires living in opposition to nature, which likens him to a robot.

It is superfluous to add that this unbridled pseudo-spirituality, the Manichean origin of which is indisputable, is fundamentally hostile to Christianity. Living according to this "spirit," one comes to refuse to incarnate spirit into life, to escape from the world where what is worthwhile is valued, and to hate the central doctrine of our faith, the

---

11   Latin, most just earth, from the *Georgics*, Book 2.
12   Latin, divide and conquer.

Incarnation. The essential task of man here below is to pursue the innate impulses of his incarnate nature, this spirit which gives him life, at each moment of his earthly existence, to let them permeate his whole being, all his acts, even to his marrow. St. Thérèse let this spirit penetrate to the very taproots of her life, and man today must begin with this, the drama of incarnation. She shows us the real, authentic ideal, the theory and practice of which are one. She points out to us that the least everyday act can enclose in itself all the light showered down from heaven. She connects the human imperative, a pure reflection of God who created it, to the divine imperative.

Thus the humble little sister, deprived of any intellectual status but provided by God with an incomparable intuition, encounters the diagnostics of Nietzsche who was at the same time like her, but on a level that was human, all too human, inhuman, a man who was both decadent, and the opposite of decadent: "We must not only endure what is necessary. . . we must also love it." "All questions of politics, the social order, and education have been falsified from the beginning, because people have been taught to despise the 'little' things, that is, all the fundamental things in life."[13]

On this infinitesimal foundation and with a superabundance of grace, the people of tomorrow will build a new civilization.

There is no civilization without a hierarchy, without an infusion of the religious and sacred which comes from certain people whose organic relationships are enfleshed in their attitudes as expressed in day-to-day life. Our era, when abstract ideologies put everyone on the same level, does not escape from this law: above devitalized people who resemble each other more and more hovers the despotism of ideas manipulated by select "organizers." Death also

13   *Ecce Homo*, 1908.

involves a hierarchy. It has its nobility: the technicians of the social machinery, and its clergy, doctrinaire philosophers and theologians of humanity.

The experience of two centuries is enough to prove that it is impossible to engage in combat, from without, against a civilization abstracted from life without being immediately tainted by it. It is quite clear that efforts to put a stop to the by-products of contemporary civilization, the political democracy, fascism and communism deriving from it, result in an increase of the evils targeted for eradication. After conquering national socialism, all nations consolidated their victory in their own milieu: an idol overcome by another idol is assured of its longevity. This principle is verified without exception in all areas of civilized life. At least some minds accept it as an obvious fact that it is futile to hope for no matter what kind of "counter-civilization," even Christian. Let us see the consequence of this, as in the parable of the wheat and the chaff, and, with fervent patience, wait for the reaping of the harvest. In an image drawn from nature, the wheat puts its roots deep into the earth and raises its stalk towards the sky in order not to be stifled by parasitic vegetation. The pressure put on people by the declining civilization requires those among them who have maintained enough strength and life in their souls to cling tightly to the twofold reality of what is here below and what is up above, to earth and heaven. The seeds they yield will do the rest.

We designate those people as the elites. The need for them to act without faltering requires them to be what they are, whether by nature or grace. When the end comes, they will be the only ones to survive, because they will have resisted. Through their vigor they will have preserved the fundamental relationship between man and the world. Once more in the course of the centuries, the utmost evil will have given birth to good. A new cycle is beginning, formed around a new aristocracy, promising both grandeur and misery. We are permitted to anticipate how it will proceed. The nobility – we are speaking of the future – is defined as its roots, and the clergy as its flower.

It is of the essence of nobility not to be able to distinguish it from the character of the one who possesses it: it is one with the person who embodies it, it penetrates him to his core. No one is less liable to duplicity than the noble soul: he unreservedly hates lies. In this sense, he belongs entirely to the vegetable kingdom in an analogical sense. While animals conceal themselves and ordinary people are fruitful in cunning, plants alone show themselves to be what they are, without the least tendency to call attention to themselves. The noble person clearly affirms himself as who he is and at the same time totally rejects egotism. Contempt for death, common to aristocrats of every kind, underlines this apparent contradiction. This explains why the noble soul behaves with a kind of innocence: like trees, he is completely incapable of depravity or crimes. His most visible characteristic is connected to this: fidelity to the roots of existence and the laws of the universe which sustain them, which elevates him above mortals in his vigorous verticality. The noble soul is essentially an upright soul rising proudly from his roots, who prefers death to the decay of the roots from which he springs. He sacrifices fortune, comfort, and life to the honor of a rectitude which is indebted to nothing except himself and the divine light. It follows that nobility is inseparable from a certain outward severity of character, present from his very birth, like the bark of a tree, designed to protect the integrity and indivisibility of his being. This results in the merging of his public and private lives, at his level of society. The kings of France were not unaware that from birth to death they lived under the eyes of their people. It is not the same with the clergy: their *character indelibilis*[14] can cover over the lack of a well-integrated personality, vice, and a thousand

---

14 Latin, indelible character or mark.

other weaknesses. (If the cleric is an integrated person, so much the better! He is then on the way to sanctity...or the opposite.) This gives us to understand clearly something proper to the clergy, which is that there is nothing more absurd than judging the priest by his private life. In one sense, the more there is of a separation between the public and private life of a priest, or rather, the greater the tension between the two that he tolerates, the more his indelible priestly character manifests itself. It is not virtue that makes the priest, but the sacred mantle which clothes him: the habit absolutely makes the monk, provided that it is not dirty, tattered, full of holes, provided that he is *hieratical.*[15] A base action can besmirch the noble; no vice can stain the priest. Today we consider that the opposite is true, and that is undoubtedly one of the most obvious signs of the decadence of the nobility and the clergy of our day.[16]

Yet if a well-integrated personality, rooted in reality, with a vertical dimension, does not constitute the human essence of the cleric, it is indispensable to understand that the anointing with sacred oil requires the priest to have other natural abilities which have nothing to do with the sap of his roots, but which are summarized above all in an intuition of the universal presence of God. The priest must have, above all, a contemplative disposition. The clergy has so few points in common with the nobility, though it is not in opposition to it, as the Church with unerring discernment takes her priests from all social classes.

We have unfortunately forgotten the essential factor, from the point of view of nature, without which the indelible supernatural character looks like mere electroplating, a bath in a certain solution; a period of time inside a greenhouse to force blossoms; or training in the externals

---

15 I.e., a priest.
16 De Corte may be referring to the failure to appreciate the sacred function of the priest, and the fact that the valid administration of the sacraments is not abrogated by his moral lapses. It must be remembered that this book was published in quite different times.

of behavior... This is the natural gift for contemplation, which can in no way be replaced by virtue, moral standards, or mode of behavior. The priest can have the virtues associated with morality, it is desirable that he have them, it is not essential for him to cultivate them to the maximum, without a call to sanctity. His mission demands above all that he be capable of *dianoetic skills* [17], which enable him to spread the word of God, as he employs them to discover and contemplate the presence of God in the human person. Here we find an explanation of the contemporary paradox regarding the clergy: immeasurably more virtuous than formerly, they are also less convincing; their morals are incomparably more pure, yet their intuition of the spiritual is much less; their ability to find God everywhere, even in the most humble circumstances, has lessened and is channeled according to their particular moral virtues; their limited power of contemplation scarcely allows them to perceive God beyond restricted spheres of life which then come into conflict with other sectors of the world and limit their zeal to evangelize.

Everything is happening as though the clergy, allied with the up-and-coming bourgeoisie, had wanted to join it in fighting against the nobility on its own ground, and, like the bourgeoisie, to have its role in society. However nothing is more difficult, if not self-contradictory, since the mission of the priest is only indirectly social. The noble is on a higher social level due to the virtues associated with his life, while the clergy is on the level of the transcendent due to his spiritual faculties. Besides, there is no society without the power to propagate, and forms of thought, the prerogative of the clergy, are just not passed down in this way. This emphasizes the innate absurdity of marriage for priests: it was so obvious that Christ never spoke of it. The concrete intervention of the priest in the

---

17 Capable of reaching conclusions through reasoning or argument, as opposed to intuition.

life of society, since his vocation itself removes him from his family and community of origin, has doubtlessly been, and still is, one of the gravest mistakes which religion has made and the source of muddled confusion, to the benefit of his adversaries. Without deep roots in society or, often, internal resources for contemplation, the priest involved in the world can be nothing other than a demagogue or dictator, often both at the same time. While the nobility is sedentary, bound to the earth, the transcendence of contemplative thought requires the cleric to remain at a distance, to maintain discretion, and when he deviates from this course, he is changed automatically into a kind of spiritual nomad, with dissembling, disavowals, and skillful maneuvering, saving face while losing his substance. Such is the great danger continually lying in wait for the priest: rupture with every form of reality, human and divine, the abrupt severing of the invisible yet solid link between the two, which enables concepts and reflections to be conveyed, the best of what he can offer. This link is broken off all at once due to the burden of a social life. The seed from a flower picked too soon never takes root.

The place of the noble and priest in the civilization which is in the preparatory stage and which cannot appear without their presence can now be outlined in broad terms.

The true nobleman will take back the place which his predecessor has deserted: he will be the mediator between man and reality, between man and his fellows. Every human being should find in him an example of being rooted and incarnate in reality. The authentic noble is the form of man in the Aristotelian sense of the word, his essence brought to perfection, which is the end to which his life is directed. The true priest is the mediator between earth and heaven. This means that he is attached to one and the other, perpetually stretched out on the cross. He is bound to heaven by the grace of ordination, to earth by his mind, not a disembodied mind, but highly spiritualized. Both orientations are necessary to him: if he is not drawn to what is here below and what is on high by being lifted up on the cross, the priest, it must be said, is worth nothing. His domain is that of contemplation where the impetus of the soul nullifies the gravity of nature. It is therefore senseless, in the full sense of the word, to conceive of the priest as a man of action, a politician, or administrator. If he holds one of those positions, it is almost always to the detriment of his human vocation, which preemptorily calls him to be a thinker. The thought of the cleric is not just concerned with studies, scholasticism, philosophy, or even theology: it is the elevation of the mind through experience of the transcendental and the universal presence of the Creator in the creature. It is precisely this contemplative power that gives him the vision needed to accomplish anything: it is a fact that the greatest accomplishments, those which have most profoundly put their stamp on the world, in the way that God fashioned creation, have been those of contemplatives. While the symbol of the noble is the man who takes hold of and palpates what is real, that of the priest is the eye, which transcends, dominates, and imposes a direction. While Aristotelian asceticism aimed at mortification of the sense of touch and the maximum adaptability, clerical asceticism must attain the greatest lucidity and the purification of thought to the level of complete impartiality. This is why the nobleman can only evolve towards increasing greatness, capable of encompassing the most extended areas, while the priest can only make progress in littleness and self-effacement. The nobleman shapes reality, while the priest acts only as leaven. The nobleman bears his responsibility — *honor onus* — ,[18] while the priest searches out all the hidden recesses of earthly fallenness.

This is also the reason why the aristocratic and ecclesiastical moral codes are different. The former is entirely in opposition to the self; it is an ethics pertaining to a

---

18   Latin, honor is a burden.

group, constituted by the relationships of its members, by the feeling of *we*, by a common destiny. It is traditional in the sense that it knows the well-tested rules for preserving one's character against the wearing effects of proximity or the passing of time: even when its sustaining roots grow old, the eminently social and personal carapace of the nobleman endures, similar to the bark, covered with moss, of an ancient tree already made hollow by death. Here everything goes from the interior towards the exterior, even when the interior is no longer anything but dust.

The priest is on the contrary autonomous, without being an individualist. One could say that each priest has his own ethical code, *since he is alone*, with his thoughts, before God. In a strange paradox, the self that through its own power attains to the level of transcendental thought – for human contemplation, and a fortiori contemplation inspired by divine grace, is not transmitted to others, except through words – must annihilate himself in order to exist: he must be taken up into and consumed by the transcendent in order to be fulfilled. This self, identified with its vision, can only see, and can only see itself, through the divine light which effaces it. No matter where he goes, the cross imprints its fiery brand on the conduct of the cleric. Here everything becomes interiorized, everything becomes the self, in a deeper way than the actual self which abandons itself so that on its wheel of execution, it might become a universal self, paradoxically full and empty. Hence the great danger of clerical psittacism[19] which mimics what is universal while emptying it of content and focusing on the self. From this point of view, there is nobody more vulnerable than the priest to conscious or unconscious pretense. This is where the void of the clerical *we* comes from. If it appears, it is what it is: a void without value. Most of the meetings of priests, of monasteries where the collective spirit dominates, are examples of this. Whence

---

19   Mechanical, repetitive, meaningless speech.

comes the ecclesiastical tendency to run with the hare and hunt with the hounds, a parody of universal breadth, freely welcoming all opinions, turning the self into a tight-rope walker. It was undoubtedly a reaction to these clerics, not faithful to their priestly office, that the dogma of the infallibility of the Supreme Pontiff was proclaimed, as he is the outstanding example of one who is alone before God.

This brief analysis brings to light the significance of the decline of the elites on both the natural and supernatural levels. The fundamental phenomenon of our civilization is the loss of the sense of the sacred among the elites themselves, and, consequently, in all of society: the river which is polluted as it descends from the mountain no longer irrigates the plain. It is appropriate here to emphasize strongly once more that it does not have to do in any way with the opinions or systems of thought professed by aristocratic and ecclesiastical elites on the social or religious level. It is a matter of an attitude which is *experienced* in the face of the social or universal, which transforms this outward attitude into an artificial, mechanical carapace or into a living organ of expression, according to the absence or the presence of the sense of the sacred. We would readily label this latter attitude as piety before the mystery of life and of the soul, but not just any piety: a piety which *works actively* under human or divine influence, and *bows down* to accept it. The sacred is not different from respect for order in the world within civilization and, so to speak, from a genuflection which emphasizes the religious character of human existence, that is to say (to avoid here confessional differences which run the risk of clouding the issue) its "non-commutative" relationship[20] with the absolute which it derives from and which it can in no way *modify*. At a certain deep level, the world can only be grasped as a kind of sacred vision, intangible in its essence, a kind of esoteric communion which constitutes the privilege and the divine

---

20 In other words, the relationship is unchanging.

gift of those whose role is to spread about, through the prestige of their example, the treasure of their experience.

This privilege does not at all come from anything one has acquired, as one acquires things, but from one's innate capacity for existence; it is not something one possesses, but something one is. In other words, it is the lived relationship of man with the sacred.

The submission to the profound order of the universe, whether natural or supernatural, in action or contemplation, establishes the aristocracy; the acceptance of physical or spiritual requisites constitutes its foundation; nothing is in harmony with destiny without being predestined. The aristocracy of the noble and of the clergy taken in this sense is a continued call to recognize the existence of the sacred, and an ontological order from which they cannot be separated without breaking off the act of communion which binds them to it, without giving rise to the temptation to lay a sacrilegious hand on it through this rupture. It is perhaps even necessary to say that the rupture of this relationship is the sacrilege par excellence.

The rupture has been produced everywhere. We have said much about it and the distinction between the sacred and profane forms of Christian civilization serves as a not insignificant indication. We contemplate with our own eyes a phenomenon which has not occurred since the fall of the ancient world: the aging of the elites who desecrate the pact made between man and the universe. The models of the active life and the contemplative life are degenerating into caricatures. The exhausted elites admit to being unable to exercise their function: just as with an individual who is worn out, their behavior evolves towards inertia or pointless restlessness. Their features become disfigured, blurred, or wasted. This twofold tendency associated with fatigue is also found in the "bourgeoisie" of money, mistress of the economy, which replaces the old, declining nobility, and in the clergy, isolated in their practice of the moral virtues or carried away by the cult of technology, activism, and the positive sciences, who have abandoned their former norm of contemplation. What is an instrument, determined by and subsumed to its end, escapes from the hands of the worker, exhausted by his work, and imposes its own law on him. Money is no more than a tool; science, with its consequences and possibilities, is only a servant. It becomes opposed to the transcendental and desecrates the soul; money becomes anti-life and desecrates life. The means which was in the hands of the elite becomes popularized, and, inasmuch as it is separated from its end in the public sphere, descends into the reserves of life and spirit which are the origin of the people and poisons them. This is life and spirit at bargain rate, within the reach of all, with consequences which the genius of the poet has discerned:

I am Everyone, *the mysterious enemy of* Everything. [21]

Yet this is only the external aspect of the disturbance which produces the sclerosis of the elites. The evil in our civilization caused by their deficiencies is infinitely more grave, and also, alas!, more unrecognized. If we were pressed to define the role of the current elites in concrete terms, we would readily say that it consists in transforming through their personal example the evils inherent in the human condition (war, sorrow, deprivation...) into greater goods, and to prevent the good things (wealth, comfort, technology, knowledge...) from degenerating into evil. The elite is placed essentially "beyond good and evil,"[22] which they purify and regulate. For every actual good projects onto the field of our earthly existence a corresponding shadow; every actual evil possesses, hidden within it, a spark of good. There is no absolute good in the world, and there is only absolute evil in a world devoid

21 *Dieu*, 1891, poem by Victor Hugo, the most celebrated French Romantic writer, 1802–1885.
22 Possibly a reference to Nietzsche's book *Beyond Good and Evil, A Prelude to a Philosophy of the Future*, 1886.

of all relationships, made unlivable. Good and evil are bound together.

Thus vertebra is joined to vertebra.

The role of the elites is to assure that throughout the civilization there is a kind of circulatory system and organic metabolism that filters out what is bad and nourishes what is good, since the meaning of the relationships which sustain the elites and an intuition of the sacred which gives them life enable them to dominate and integrate opposites into a synthesis, like a healthy body which processes a variety of foods.

Historical experience, like recent events, shows us only too well the impotence of the elites in carrying out their task, due to their decrepitude. We see them hold on to their outward privileges, without being able to carry out their primary role. Civilization, which is inserted into the domain of the relative and, because it is earthbound, cannot attain to the absolute, is immobilized in its great inefficacious efforts. This is a permanent revolution: evils remain evils or become worse, good things are debased, and the polar relationship between good and evil, since it is not overcome, ruptures. At the same time, as the commerce between relatively good and evil things is no longer operative, the passion for an absolute good or an absolute evil attainable here below invades the souls of people. Civilization becomes at once nihilistic and mystical.

One must not be surprised that the elites are growing old: this occurs at each major turning point of a civilization where, during a slack period of transition, there are preparations for a renewal, without which no human life would be possible. The exhausted elites cut themselves off from the people, in Péguy's meaning of the word, [23] when

---

23 Péguy believed in the excellence of the French people, with their sense of honor, the value of hard work, and decency. See, for example, *Par ce demi-clair matin*, 1952.

these are being reinvigorated and reborn. The history of the nobility under royal absolutism in the eighteenth century, of the bourgeoisie absorbed into the mechanical rhythm of production in the nineteenth and twentieth centuries, and finally of people today sapped of life by political parties, map out the battle lines of this process of senescence where the advantages of authority, technology, and the foundations of social order among the people are no longer operative. The good ineluctably changes into its opposite.

☙

I am not going to prophesy. There are, however, some concrete conditions which preside over the appearance of the elites, which allow us to probe into the future. Every aristocracy arises from the people, in the full meaning of the word: people living organically according to the laws governing their natural groupings, independent of human manipulation. As long as these popular nuclei remain, they will still be able to re-create the nobility and clergy, or, more exactly, to produce new types of them.

The evolution of contemporary society is working paradoxically in this way: the rise of the masses eliminates the "bourgeoisie" and makes a new nobility possible; the subservience of science to the state dethrones the scientist and makes a new clergy possible if their original roots continue to live in a subterranean manner.

The future nobility will undoubtedly return to its origins, working the land or engaged in other work, the clergy to its disinterested transcendental thoughts. Everything in the direction taken by the modern world contributes to isolate them, to constrain them to a *recollected solitude*. Universal demagogy and anti-religious sentiment, both on the increase, in some way make them stand out, and prepare them for their great work of the future. The hand and the eye, forced to be no more than hand and eye, are going to be purified. If a new civilization appears, it will have its nobility and clergy: these must then be born in the very conditions of a dying civilization, and, according to all probability, this will be imposed on them, since the construction of the civilization of the future will be their work. Just as the noble of medieval civilization is the remote product of the man *corpori adnexus et glebae adscriptus*[24] of the edict of Diocletian,[25] the noble of the new civilization will arise from the rigid communities created by the modern state, from which he will not possibly be able to escape in this life, as does the weak nobility of today. The future priest will be born out of a situation where science is reduced to servitude by the state; he will be brought back to his true functional role. The new nobility will arise from the family, forced to lead a settled life, the new clergy from man leading a hidden life deep within the catacombs of the world, restricted to solitary thought and meditation on the state of the world. New roots will develop. A visionary clergy, a new leaven, with a new impartial, contemplative eye, will be present.

There is always a cycle: the two extremes come together. From the utmost misery in an era of increasing organization of society, in which we are imprisoned, the tiny seed of a future civilization is developing. The old cycle has to run its course before a new cycle can begin. Time does not matter: the seed which is preserved, patiently awaiting the advent of light, is scornful of time. It is only important to preserve the seed: this is our only task, incomparably more active than any dramatic action which then returns to the obscurity of night, with all lanterns extinguished. A fable, in the style of Plato, will tell us about it, recounted

---

24   Latin, incorporated into his station in society and tied to the land.
25   In 301 the Roman emperor Diocletian issued his Edict on Maximum Prices in an effort to control inflation. To curb the resulting flight from Rome, he and his successors attempted to tie people to the land, establishing serfdom.

by an old peasant of genius. He shows us a deed of enduring value, unforgettable, sprung from a superabundance of contemplation and resilient roots. Such an act does not die.

Here it is. It has to do with *Derborence*.[26] Some shepherds went up to the mountain with their flocks to spend the summer in their chalets, rising above the clouds. One night, the mountain behind the sheepfold collapses. Just one shepherd escapes from the avalanche. Buried beneath a huge mass of rocks for two months, he lives on dry bread and water seeping from the debris. He probes into the rocks and hollows a way out, at times feeling defeated but always persisting. He comes out, speechless, stammering, spectral. For he wants to live: his home awaits him. He goes down to the village, where the people are startled before this phantom. The priest goes to meet him armed with a cross. His wife approaches. "And after looking at him closely, though at a distance, as though she dared not draw near, said,

"'Oh! Antoine is it you?'

"'Just touch me, this is my skin, my flesh, now that I have borne the cross . . . Just touch me,' he said, 'You'll see, I'm not an invention of your mind, I'm solid, I won't go away, it's me.'

"'Oh!' she said, 'Is it possible?'"

The future belongs to saints and heroes, at once visible and invisible. We just have to open our eyes.

---

26 Novel by Charles Ferdinand Ramuz, 1936.

ABOUT THE AUTHOR

MARCEL DE CORTE was born in Belgium in 1905 and died in 1994. Philosopher, heir to the great Aristotelian tradition, contemporary of Jacques Maritain, Étienne Gilson, Gabriel Marcel, and Gustave Thibon, he taught at the University of Liège until 1975. Frequent contributor to the Catholic periodical, *Itinéraires,* and author of more than twenty works on philosophical reflection, he was notably interested in social evolutions that stem from the French and Industrial Revolutions, principally regarding the moral and social disintegration of modern man.